The Presbyterian Source

Also by Louis B. Weeks

Making Ethical Decisions: A Casebook

To Be a Presbyterian

Kentucky Presbyterians

The Presbyterian Source

Bible Words That Shape a Faith

Louis B. Weeks

Westminster/John Knox Press
Louisville, Kentucky

Book design by DeskTop Services, Inc.

First edition

Published by Westminster/John Knox Press
Louisville, Kentucky

PRINTED IN THE UNITED STATES OF AMERICA
9 8 7 6 5 4 3

Library of Congress Cataloging-in-Publication Data

Weeks, Louis B., 1941–
The Presbyterian source : Bible words that shape a faith / Louis B. Weeks. — 1st ed.
p. cm.
ISBN 0-664-25100-5

1. Presbyterian Church—Doctrines. 2. Bible—Study. I. Title.
BX9175.2.W42 1990
230'. 5—dc20 89-29548
CIP

Contents

1

The Invitation and the Responsibility

"How can we be Presbyterians if we don't know the Bible? How can we be Christians at all?" She pointed her finger at me, but she spoke of her own ignorance and of the lack of knowledge among members of her congregation. "We claim to be people of the Book! I'm afraid for us Presbyterians it's just the *Book of Order,* if we have any book at all."

Deeply committed, caring, and well educated otherwise, this woman in Charlotte, North Carolina, put her finger on a real problem among Presbyterian Christians. In her words, "Bible study attracts us, but we don't apply our learnings and they wash off like water off a duck's back."

As fifty of us talked during a workshop on Presbyterian identity, it became clear that while some knew the Bible quite well and drew upon it, others did not have much grasp of the scriptures.

I find the same situation in most places where I teach and preach, among synods and presbyteries, in congregations across the country, and at home in our particular church. We even find some students beginning seminary with only a superficial acquaintance with scripture.

At one Presbytery Day in Dayton, Ohio, a man told me, "You ought to write a book to help us study the Bible while we study who we are as Presbyterians." At the time I thought of the many good resources that exist for Bible study, and I named some for him. Later, however, I realized he offered me an invitation, for I could find no Bible study that also consciously focused on Presbyterian development.

In a manner of speaking, our Christian lives are full of invitations and responsibilities. The most important invitation is the one to believe the gospel. The same God who created the whole universe invites us through Jesus Christ to become heirs of the kingdom. Accepting that invitation, we share in the responsibility to proclaim the word of salvation and service, to seek to grow in love for God and others, and to respond in praise and thanksgiving.

Other invitations and responsibilities flow from those primary ones. Invitations call us to the work we undertake, the relationships we nurture, and the decisions we make. Real responsibilities flow from such work, relationships, and decisions. Through such a chain of invitations and responsibilities, I came to accept the invitation of the Presbyterian colleague in Dayton, and I offer this study book for him as well as for the woman in Charlotte. Though I am a Bible scholar only in the broadest sense of the phrase, I have studied the Bible in order to interpret it as a teaching elder in the church. I also study scripture both for devotional purposes and to help me better understand Presbyterian history.

I take responsibility for helping others learn about our tradition and, in this vein, offer a study to help all of us learn more about scripture.

I also pass along words of both invitation and responsibility to the reader. Please study the Bible as you study these selections from it and my insights about our heritage. I can promise the serious study of scripture will be rewarding. Knowing how our tradition has used the Bible will be a guide along the way.

Please consider the study of the Bible as part of your life as well as part of your faith. I fear that people today, even

Christian people, frequently do not apply the resources of scripture in their living and in their dying. According to our heritage, God gave us the Bible to provide for us "all that pertains to a saving faith" (Second Helvetic Confession 5.002).

Please share your learnings with others, and your study will become more firmly planted personally. I really worry that in this era we tend to assume experts alone know things well. Yet the Protestant Reformation began and built on the confidence that all would know the Bible and share in teaching it. For that reason, spreading literacy to all has been especially important in the Reformed tradition. Education in general has been encouraged, for study of other subjects helps ministers and lay leaders understand the Bible better.

As one branch of the church emerged and came to call itself "Reformed," it put special emphasis on knowing scripture. Reformed Christians considered the whole of scripture important for the church—Old Testament as well as New, wisdom writings and law as well as prophets and Gospels.

As we shall see, Presbyterian churches grew from that Reformed wing of Protestantism. Through the centuries since the sixteenth, no other branch of the Christian family has put more importance on the Bible, though some have claimed to. Before looking at our Presbyterian heritage further, let us think together about the Bible in more detail.

An Authority That Does Not Oppress

My friend John Mulder, the president of the seminary I serve, sums up the modern Presbyterian dilemma in the words of a member of the Highland Presbyterian Church, in Louisville, who said in a discussion, "I seek something to hold onto in this topsy-turvy world, an authority—but one that does not oppress me."

That Presbyterian put her finger on precisely the appeal of scripture for sixteenth-century Reformers. They found

God's authority in the Bible, which contrasted with the oppressive power of human beings controlling church and state.

For those who seek in the Bible a blueprint of the past or a recipe for prosperity, traditional Presbyterian interpretations remain frustrating. Reformed Christians have labeled as idolatry such superficial formulas for understanding the Bible. We call that worship of the Bible "bibliolatry."

We Presbyterians believe that the Bible points through its authority to the power of God, and that the Spirit, who provides at first milk from scripture, in time nourishes the mature Christian with a full diet.

Scripture offered everyone who could read it the good news of God's grace. It called people to God. It provided a lifetime of riches for learning and growing as a "saint." If cars had been invented in the sixteenth century, the Reformers' slogan might have been proclaimed on bumper stickers: SOLA GRATIA, SOLA FIDES, SOLA SCRIPTURA (grace alone, faith alone, scripture alone).

"Whom can you trust?" they would ask. "Will you grant authority to those men in Rome? Or will you give authority to this, God's word, which is right here for you?"

In affirming the priesthood of all believers, Reformers translated the Bible into the languages of all peoples. They committed themselves to teaching everyone to read the Bible. In truly amazing numbers, men and women, boys and girls took up the Bible, which they saw as so important, and learned to read it. Many of them even memorized vast portions of it.

How much has the world changed since then, especially in the past few decades? Our family frequently discusses whether human beings today are different from those in past generations. In some ways we probably have changed very little, but Christians as well as others in recent decades have changed drastically in our habits of reading and learning. In the 1800s, for very good reasons, Christians and others developed more efficient printing presses and new ways of distributing books and papers cheaply. As a result, those of us in recent generations have had many more things to read than did early Presbyterians.

In recent decades we have quantified reading speeds and even taught ourselves to "scan" for a certain measure of "comprehension." Have you heard about the graduate of the speed-reading course who was asked by her teacher if she had read the novel *War and Peace*? "Yes," she replied. "I read it in thirty minutes." "What is it about?" the teacher asked. The response: "Russia."

Television, of course, has increased this tendency to think we know something if we see it quickly and then go on to other things. We seldom read with *devotion* to the task.

In previous generations, families might own only a few books: the Bible, a psalter, a copy of *Pilgrim's Progress*, perhaps Foxe's *Book of Martyrs*, and a few others. Members of the family would read the books aloud to one another, and then they would talk about what they read.

Naturally such family reading, especially of the Bible, gave to the work a certain authority. We might better say that God's Spirit provided a sense of authority for scripture through its being read and discussed frequently and with great care.

Our tendency to seek easy and superficial learning has inclined many of us to believe all learning occurs at about the same level. I find theories of the "literal truth" of scripture or of its "verbal inspiration" superficial and mechanical. No one who has a change of clothes believes entirely that the Bible should be followed word for word. Everyone interprets the Bible, even the saying of Jesus that we should give our cloaks also to those who ask for our coats (Matt. 5:40). But interpreting the Bible calls for a level of learning and thought that is different from scanning the headlines of the day.

The Bible can have much more authority for us as we

come to know it better. It can be, if it is not already, "an authority that does not oppress."

Study of the Bible Today

Each of us knows mature Christians who seem to radiate genuine and deep knowledge of the Bible. To introduce a new curriculum, I recently shared the thinking of five such people, all serious students of scripture.

I'll never forget the story Mary Alice Hays told about learning the Bible. She spoke of her own mother and of growing up in a small town on the banks of the Ohio River. "Mother would tell Bible stories *from her own experience,*" Mary Alice joked. "I learned from her the wealth of meaning and the depth of scriptural truth. When new things came along—zoology courses at college, for example, or the civil rights campaigns—those Bible stories I knew first from Mother's sharing them and then from reading them myself kept me on an even keel."

I asked Mary Alice Hays about the nature of her Bible study, and she smiled. "It's nothing fancy, I assure you—just the asking of the questions who, what, when, where, and how?" Friends who have shared Bible study with Mary Alice Hays say that is exactly how she teaches the Bible. She focuses on the questions and invites discussion.

In a manner of speaking, Mary Alice Hays invites people to study scripture from both outside and inside. That responsibility to participate as well as to understand becomes clearer as life proceeds. We ask some questions as "outsiders" who want to understand, but I will ask in the next chapter for us also to study the Reformed heritage as "insiders," as those who share it.

The question "Who?" is the question of authorship and whose words are used. Some might call it the question of persons. Who speaks? Is God speaking? To whom? Is the word addressed to everyone, to believers, to the prophet, or to the close disciple?

The question "What?" is the question of content. Strangely, we sometimes pay less attention to what the passage says than we do to other elements of study. Yet what is actually said may be most important for us.

"When?" asks about time and context of the scripture. Commentaries and dictionaries of the Bible can give this helpful information quickly.

"Where?" can be a very specific question sometimes, very general at other times.

"How?" is the question of form. Is the word a teaching, an account of something happening, a law, a poem, a tall tale, a parable? Truth lies in all these forms, but it comes to us differently depending on the style. And the word has substance, but what kind? Reformed Christians have usually been smart enough to discern that teachings, laws, and parables do not bear the same authority.

To these general questions my friend and colleague Gene March suggests a sixth: "So what?" What did the passage mean for people then and how does it apply to us right here and now?

Those six questions offer a good starting point for Bible study. It also helps to consider the whole of scripture in listening to a part of it. That advice becomes more important as we gain a "sense of scripture" after much study.

Another helpful piece of advice comes from John Calvin, who said to let scripture interpret scripture; let the simple parts help in understanding the more difficult. Calvin also said that Christians can find a lifetime of riches in the study of just the most simple, obvious portions of scripture.

The various parts of scripture have been included in the Bible for many reasons. The Spirit working through the writers of books of the Bible worked through those who brought together portions of the Bible. That same Spirit, we believe, helps us learn from scripture.

In your study of the Bible, you can rely on that Spirit to inform you, to help you grow in knowledge and devotion.

You will want to read the passages, perhaps to read some other portions of scripture that bear on them, and to allow other Christians to teach you as you teach others.

I find Bible study in groups much more appealing if responsibilities are shared—assigning various questions to members of the group, for example, or asking some to focus on application of the learning.

In this Bible study, I will help you address the six questions and use some of these other guides too. I will also tell you some personal stories and share illustrations that tie the Bible to my own life and growth. I hope they will help rather than detract from your study of scripture.

Before looking at particular passages, however, let us inspect for a bit our Presbyterian perspective on scripture. What is our identity in Reformed Christianity?

2

A Presbyterian Identity

It came as an embarrassing question several years ago. I had been holding forth on the history and beliefs of Presbyterians for an adult class at the Faith Church in Valley Station, Kentucky. The members listened patiently, until one could take it no longer and blurted out, "Why should we worry about keeping Christianity Reformed"—she paused to get the right phrase—"in an ecumenical age?"

I confess I stammered at the time. I felt the desire to defend my Presbyterian version of the Christian faith, but why? What is the value of a Presbyterian "way," when we see other Christians have a portion of the truth as well?

After much thought and study, I am convinced there is value in the Presbyterian way. Reformed Christianity and the Presbyterian church in it keep nourishing me well and feed my soul. I find this is true for many others, both those raised in the tradition and those who have chosen it along their pilgrimages.

I have begun to write articles and books on the subject and to address it in congregations and larger gatherings of Presbyterians. I have learned from members of the church by asking about their faith and Reformed distinctiveness in it. Many Presbyterians do ask for help in speaking about any special identity we share.

For a Bible study, and maybe in every situation, the first word is that Presbyterians are Christians. We are members of the body of Christ, the whole universal church.

The apostle Paul, whose theology has proven extremely important for Presbyterians, said the Christian should "put on Christ." A Christian identity could and should become the identity of the believer. In the words of the Gospel, "Let your light so shine . . . that [others] may see your good works and give glory to your Father" (Matt. 5:16).

Those who sought to reform the Christian church, especially those in the sixteenth century, did not just mimic the early church of the New Testament. Rather, they tried to be faithful to the spirit of that earliest community of Christians. Reformers who started the Reformed wing of Protestantism went even further. They claimed a continuity between the people of God in the Old Testament and the Christian movement in the New Testament. Presbyterians have tried to be faithful to the spirit of both, to depend on God's Spirit for understanding and the power to do what is God's will. We try to order our worship and work today similar to the ways they ordered their worship and work.

Where did the major doctrines come from—the sovereignty of God, the sinfulness of humanity, the incarnation of Jesus Christ, the salvation of people for eternal life, and even election and predestination? These doctrines came right from the center of scripture. Nobody made them up.

Theological emphases in scripture became the basis for church reform, including the Protestant reform of the sixteenth century. Our branch of the Protestant family has emphasized the need to keep thinking about the faith, to keep interpreting it anew in changing situations. We fondly quote the summary of the law: to "Love God with all your *mind*. . . ."

Granted our common characteristics with all Christians, what characterizes our Presbyterian heritage?

Elements in Reformed Christianity

If we listen to the Bible and its reading through the church we find some teachings at its core—God's sovereignty, human sinfulness, the incarnation of Jesus Christ, the promise that God's Spirit would be with those who believe, the promise of eternal life, human responsibility for the world, the need to proclaim the gospel, and more. All Christians hear these teachings and interpret them in different ways.

Is there a distinctive mix of teachings for Presbyterians? I believe so. Exploring that mix would take another whole book, but you can do it as you study the Bible itself. Ask among your own family and your friends. Listen to sermons and offerings at presbytery level. Here is a brief outline of some obvious starting points:

God's godness, or God's sovereignty, underlies Presbyterian theology, as it does the theology of most other portions of the Christian family. That's where the Bible starts, and the assertions of Genesis will begin our Bible study. The whole Bible keeps teaching that God is God. No other will finally prevail.

The incarnation of Jesus Christ means that Jesus Christ lived as fully human while fully divine. Jesus came as the Messiah expected in Israel, the Suffering Servant called for by Isaiah, and the fulfillment of God's promises throughout the Bible. Jesus Christ lived to teach us, died to save us, and rose again to conquer death.

The Spirit of God, which is also called *the Spirit of Christ* and the Holy Spirit, came fulfilling God's promises and those made by Jesus Christ before death. Through the power of the Spirit, we can hear, believe, and proclaim the gospel. Through the work of the Spirit, the Christian movement began and continues as the body of Christ, the church.

"*Nobody's perfect* except Jesus." A young man in a confirmation class made this remarkable statement some years ago. Here lies a central word about humanity, according to our reading of the Bible. Moreover, we Presbyterians recognize that the church and its parts can sin as well as other institutions can. Presbyterians have seen God calling—through the Bible—for people and institutions to become better even when sin continues as a powerful force in them.

Human beings are responsible for the whole creation, especially for the people, lands, and institutions of which we are particular members. Christians have been called not only to believe in Jesus Christ, but also to follow in service and sacrifice. Corporate responsibility belongs to the church, to the political and social institutions, and Christians should participate in them and lead them.

Our lives should praise God, and we focus worship—both corporately and individually—with prayer, psalms, and reading and listening together to God's word proclaimed. Praise also occurs in all our living, in our family relationships, among colleagues, and everywhere.

These are just a few of the central emphases in Reformed Christianity. Our confessions and creeds center on these truths. But what about predestination, election, and other "old favorites" of Presbyterian theology? They also came from the Bible and helped Reformed Christians understand the nature of God and of ourselves; we will study these teachings too.

Presbyterian Contributions to World Christianity

We listen to the whole of the Bible. At its best, Reformed Christianity has a special way of being in the world. Presbyterians and others who share the heritage, for example, have tended to pay attention to the whole of the Bible. Most parts of the Christian family give less importance to the Old Testament, and some even say parts of the New Testament such as the Gospels are the core of the Bible.

In a Presbyterian church, a lesson or sermon can focus on Micah or Job or Proverbs without apology. Our theology has been drawn from the whole of scripture—even the tough parts for us to hear or understand. Several passages of scripture that have been most influential are harsh words of judgment, as well as many passages that speak sweet words of hope for us.

Our paying positive attention to all of scripture seems to me to be the reason we bear a distinctive theology, a particular form of church government, and a particular (if not even "peculiar") way of living. Our witness to all of scripture as authority seems also the most important contribution we can make to the rest of Christianity. That characteristic also makes it especially hard to choose the passages for our study in this book!

We Presbyterians are preoccupied with the education of all. Some might call us "obsessed" with education. Look around at the members of almost any Presbyterian congregation and see our deep involvement in literacy projects, school systems, and public libraries. Historically, we have come to honor education by knowing that each person has to hear the gospel, that reading the Bible in one's own language is necessary, and that God is Lord of all constructive knowledge.

We Presbyterians have pioneered in sharing church leadership. Most parts of the Christian family depend on clerical leadership—priests and bishops. Some other parts, such as most Mennonite and Baptist denominations, govern with lay leadership primarily. Presbyterians, emphasizing an educated ministry and an educated whole people of God, rely on a sharing of power between ministers and elders.

We Reformed Christians have also pioneered in exploring the meaning of pluralism and diversity. We Presbyterians learned early, in America especially, many lessons in politics and corporate manners; we learned to cooperate, to lobby, to seek gains for others while helping ourselves.

Equally important, Presbyterians formed an American tradition composed of several different ethnic strains. Scots, Scotch-Irish, British, Welsh, French, Dutch, German Reformed, and African-American Christians all had a profound effect in the early decades of Presbyterian life in what has become the United States of America. Subsequently, Native American, Hispanic, Hungarian, and Asian Presbyterians have become important and contributed significantly to the communion.

We Presbyterians are transformers of the culture in which we live. Other Christians embody this perspective also, but Presbyterian work in so many areas of society, politics, and culture remains extremely important. In matters of Sabbath observance, temperance, political reform, child labor laws, freedom to dissent, civil rights, and peace we have tried to influence social habits and enforce basic human morality, even at the risk of being misunderstood.

These emphases we Presbyterians may share with other parts of the whole church, but they are down deep in our faith and come out in our living. These contributions seem important, and we have the responsibility to study and to share them as we proclaim the gospel.

Studying the Heritage

We share a rich heritage indeed. It includes both Bible and Christian history. Reformed Christians consider the call of Abraham and Sarah a call to us. The life of God's people has been our life—with the judges, under the monarchy, in exile, and in restoration. Again, we see in the stories about Jesus Christ, the disciples, and the crowds, the truth about ourselves. We remember the death and resurrection of Jesus Christ at times of our faithlessness, our amazement, and our belief. In the early church, as our Bible formed, in the oppression of Christians and the easy movement into power of Christian leaders around Constantine, we see ourselves.

The study of our heritage involves us as participants, not as disinterested observers or distant analysts. In a way we stand outside the text as we ask the six questions: "Who?"

"What?" "When?" "Where?" "How?" and "So what?" and as we interpret the Bible, but we also stand inside it as a part of the family, a "cousin" if not indeed a son or daughter.

In our confessions and creeds we affirm the "communion of the saints," and we stand with them—they stand with us—in our study. They too struggled to know more about God, themselves, and the purposes of life. Long before Reformed Christianity existed in churches, Augustine wrestled with the Bible. How could one be faithful without falling into legalism on the one hand or anarchy on the other? We Presbyterians keep asking that question.

That sense of being "inside" scripture, and of working alongside readers from all the ages of the church, cannot really be expressed in words. But the study of our heritage supposes it.

Perhaps because we Presbyterians have taken the whole Bible seriously, the selection of just a few passages for our study seemed almost impossible. I have chosen basic ones, ones leaders and confessions have quoted frequently. I also asked friends to list basic passages, and I have used some they suggested.

Finally, I have arranged the study of these passages to move through the Bible, rather than organizing the study by themes. The purpose of all these decisions is to provide you with a better biblical place to stand. These passages all remain central for us, good for basic study.

We Presbyterians, who believe God is sovereign, also believe God loves and cares for all of us. God's providence leaves no room for "luck" or "fate" as separate areas of power. So I joke with you when I wish you "good luck." I am serious, however, when I say, "God be with you."

3

God Created
Genesis 1:1—3:24

Early Sunday morning on the beach: what a glorious way to begin the day, walking along in wet sand, greeting gulls and finding new shells from the night's tide! We laugh at the wavering tracks of a female loggerhead turtle who has deposited her eggs and slogged her way back to the ocean. Soon we will dress for church, and then we will greet human friends. Our voices will be full in praise today, and a primordial prayer forms as we walk along.

Gulls and loggerheads, whelks and sand and sea all invoke a sense of awe and perspective. "Who are we that God pays attention to us?" That was the cry of the psalmist. Biblical accounts of creation reflect that awe and that sense of perspective. Who made all of this? And the mountains, plains, and deltas?

God did: the same God who made us and calls us to service and salvation.

The Words of Genesis

In the beginning God created the heavens and the earth. The earth was without form and void, and darkness was upon the face of the deep; and the Spirit of God was moving over the face of the waters.

> And God said, "Let there be light," and there was light. And God saw that the light was good; and God separated the light from the darkness. God called the light Day, and the darkness God called Night. And there was evening and there was morning, one day.
>
> Genesis 1:1–5

The Bible does not start with an argument about God's existence. Nor does it start by telling about human potential. It starts with a narrative about God's creation of everything.

God made heavens and earth, light and dark, dry land and oceans, plants, stars, a sun and a moon, fish, birds, other animals, and human beings, male and female. The good Lord made them all, as the song says, and God pronounced them "good" (1:1—2:4a).

In recent decades, Christian scholars have come to see that a second account, beginning with Genesis 2:4b, gives a different perspective. The more vivid and exuberant second story reflects a simpler language style in Hebrew. God not only speaks to make things, God also does other things: caused the rain, formed a human being, breathed life, separated a rib from the man to make the woman, and talked to them about their living conditions. Students of the Bible speculate that this more humanlike description of God's work in creation was the earlier version. Later on, as the people of God focused on the "Word of God," they emphasized God speaking even to make the creation.

Despite the differences between the two narratives, both emphasize God's work in creation. Human beings have places of responsibility, but "The earth is the LORD's and the fullness thereof" (Ps. 24:1). People can look "through" the creation to God, or at least we can see God's handiwork in all of it.

The creation stories emphasize God's care for the creation. God did not leave the new beings and structures to themselves. God gave sustenance as well as form to all things.

In God's Image, Yet Fallen

All too quickly we jump from the creation to the story of the serpent, the fruit tree, the nature of sin, and sin's consequences (ch. 3). Genesis itself helps us turn quickly to look at ourselves, and even chapter 1 speaks of our being created "in the image of God," male and female.

How long can we stand just to think about God? Not very long! Like staring into a bright light, we turn away quickly. Just so we move to more manageable subjects, even if they are our own shortcomings.

Sin is there in the Genesis narrative, and it is real. Was it pride, people thinking they knew better than God what they should do? Was the initial sin idolatry, people putting knowledge or something concrete like a tree or its fruit before praise and obedience to God? Was the sin sexual in nature? Scholars and regular Christians, too, have debated the issue since the writing of Genesis.

Genesis connects sin and the fall of human beings with consequences—curses and exile. Human sinfulness affected all of life, and life grew difficult and transitory. Note that God still provided for Adam and Eve (3:21). In the sequence, then, Genesis tells of God, of the majesty of creation, of the making of human beings, and of human sin. Genesis later begins the story of God's promises to even a fallen humanity (8:20–22).

How can human beings be both in the "image" of God and also fallen in sin? That quandary has plagued God's people from the beginning. Reformed Christianity has responded by emphasizing both human sin and human responsibility.

God Sovereign and Caring

This beginning of scripture makes a good place to start talking about Presbyterian emphases. The majesty of God who made everything, the creation of people in God's image, the fallen nature of humanity, and the promises of God are all major emphases for Reformed Christians. These are "fundamentals" of our faith, together with conventions about the nature of Jesus Christ, about the work of the Holy Spirit, and about our life together in light of God's plan for us.

John Calvin, one who helped interpret Reformed Christianity, said, "Let us not be ashamed to take pious delight in the works of God open and manifest in this most beautiful theater." This world provides "first evidence in the order of nature" that all things are "works of God" (Inst. 1.14.20). The chief evidence for faith, according to Calvin, exists in scripture.

Visiting pastors from the Presbyterian Church in Korea recently asked about fundamentalism in the United States. I tried to explain that some American Christians believe five doctrines are central to the Christian faith—the inerrancy of the Bible, the deity of Christ, the virgin birth of Jesus Christ, the miracles as the Bible describes them, and the resurrection of the body. Of course, some Christians in Korea are also fundamentalists, holding the same or similar beliefs.

I said that though some Presbyterians believe in those doctrines especially, most are fundamentalists of a different sort. And several of the Presbyterian fundamentals come from Genesis 1:1 and other passages like it (1:3, 1:6). Presbyterians historically have centered on God's sovereignty, on human sinfulness, and on the importance of God's promises. We also have concentrated on the fact that Jesus Christ is God incarnate, both human and divine, not just on Christ's divinity. And we have focused on the authority of the Bible rather than on its being "perfect."

Just as the Bible has more than five central teachings, so we have emphasized a number of teachings as being very important. More than that, we claim Christians are saved by faith and by grace alone—not by holding some special doctrines in a particular way.

God's godness, God's final control over all creation,

almost all Christians confess. But for Presbyterians this primary belief has influenced behavior, prayer life, and the rest of theology. Do we still believe nothing happens outside God's final control? Do we live in confidence that God cares for us—all of us on this earth?

"Idol Factories"

Sometimes we might confuse the creation with God. At other times we place our confidence in people or in institutions to take care of us. We may believe we do not need God any longer. All these are sins, according to Reformed Christianity. And sin sneaks up on all of us all the time.

John Calvin claimed we human beings are all "idol factories." We keep making idols to try to overcome God's power and provision for us. As we mature in the faith, we discard the sillier idols, yet we cannot help making false gods of some kind. That is the truth of Genesis alongside the words about God's nature.

In traditional language, Presbyterians spoke of "original sin" and "total depravity." I like the "idol factory" image better because it speaks of our propensity to sin that does not go away. We shall look at this self-understanding again, for it remains difficult for us to see—especially about ourselves!

A Natural Order?

Some Christians worry that science leads people away from God, that scientific versions of the order of creation, the relationships among the animals, and the place of human beings in the universe according to science pose alternatives to the Bible. To these Christians the theories about the beginnings of the universe, the theories of evolution, and the manipulation of life-forms as in genetic engineering are demonic.

Other Christians sometimes worship a "God of the gaps," believing science explains part of the world and God explains the rest. God makes miracles, but an order of things exists apart from God's direction.

Presbyterians and most other Reformed Christians historically have not taken such negative views of human learning. Most of us have believed God gives scientific knowledge, just as God gives other kinds of beauty; God gives a regularity and patterns to the universe and to life-forms in it. God calls us to learn more about the universe, and the sciences offer knowledge, which may come from God.

Because God made the whole creation, did God also make an order for things? Are the sciences uncovering laws God has instituted? Reformed Christians have considered the question, and most have decided that God does offer us insights through laws of nature.

Do the laws of nature lead us to know more about God? Most have thought they do. Physics, biology, astronomy, anatomy, and other disciplines have grown especially from a Reformed way of looking at the world. Many of the human sciences—especially sociology—began with determined efforts by Christians to improve the lot of neighbors through discerning God's plan for all the human race.

Yet the natural order cannot save us. That accompanying, sobering word comes from the Reformed heritage as well.

4

Out of the House of Bondage
Exodus 20:1–17

"Lord, forgive us. . . ." We pray with our heads bowed, reading together a confession of sin. It's how we pray early in worship services at Anchorage Presbyterian, my home church. I always add some words of personal confession during that part of the service, asking forgiveness for the hurt caused to others by my actions and by my not caring.

After the confession, a minister or lay leader assures us of God's pardon to those who confess and believe in Jesus Christ. Then the leader tells us about God's law. Occasionally we read the Ten Commandments together, but more often the leader will simply recite the summary of the law from the Gospel: "You shall love the Lord your God with all your heart, and with all your soul, and with all your mind, and with all your strength." This is the first and greatest commandment. And the second, "You shall love your neighbor as yourself" (Mark 12:30, 31).

Most Protestants do not have these parts of worship, and I realize many Presbyterian congregations do not share this habit either. But it does fit Reformed use of the Bible and our understanding of God's way of caring for us.

God's Liberating and Leading

We sometimes think of God in terms of distance from ourselves. The Bible does not show God that way very much. Mostly, it portrays God leading people, talking with them, helping them in times of need. Reformed Christianity has sometimes gotten a bad name for its emphasis on God's sovereignty. But at our best, we have paid attention to God's leading and freeing people all the time.

Our confessions do not portray God as simply starting things. God did not wind the world up and then just let go and watch it. God did not leave us in our selfishness and sin. Rather God kept, and keeps, leading us out of slavery. No wonder the second book of the Bible is named "Exodus"!

Exodus shows both a series of events and a process for God's caring. The people of God have always looked back and remembered times of delivery and special help.

> I am the LORD your God, who brought you out of the land of Egypt, out of the house of bondage. You shall have no other gods before me.
>
> Exodus 20:2–3

The book of Exodus tells the story of God's freeing a chosen people and leading them to a promised land. Though the people rebelled, God kept the promises and persisted in caring for them. Exodus 20:2 recalls that process of liberation and care, God's grace. The "law" existed for them within that context, whether remembered in Exodus or in the other location of the Ten Commandments, Deuteronomy 5:6–21.

These commandments, also called traditionally the "Ten Words" or "decalogue," formed a core for other commandments given in Exodus, and especially in Leviticus and Deuteronomy. Amid cultures that permitted human slavery and considered women and children the possessions of men, the Ten Words and the other commands sought to protect all, especially those of less power and authority. Unconditional laws demanded obedience by all people, in the name of God. The laws also forbade idols.

The Ten Words

Most Bible scholars say the core of the Ten Commandments must be very old indeed. Hebrew religion might even have drawn on previous laws. Ten words, ten fingers. Every mother's child could remember them. They all began with pithy phrases that anyone could remember. In Hebrew, one just says "No kill!" and "No steal!"

The first group describes relations with God: "Have no other gods before me"; no graven images; do not take God's name in vain; and keep the Sabbath holy. We Presbyterians count these as the first four commandments.

The second group describes our lives with others: "Honor your father and your mother"; "You shall not kill"; "You shall not commit adultery"; "You shall not steal"; do not "bear false witness"; and do not covet. We consider these as the other six.

The full text has been very important for us Presbyterians historically, and our catechisms have asked children and adults to both recite the commandments and to explain what each commandment means.

Most of the answers tell a lot about healthy Christian life. In the Heidelberg Catechism, for example, question 110 asks, "What does God forbid in the eighth commandment?" Listen to the answer:

> He forbids not only the theft and robbery which civil authorities punish, but God also labels as theft all wicked tricks and schemes by which we seek to get for ourselves our neighbor's goods, whether by force or

> under the pretext of right, such as false weights and measures, deceptive advertising or merchandising, counterfeit money, exorbitant interest, or any other means forbidden by God. He also forbids all greed and misuse and waste of his gifts.

Various families of Christians divide the Ten Commandments in different ways. Catholics, for example, consider the honoring of father and mother part of the first table, while Luther considered "Have no other gods . . ." and "do not make graven images . . ." as one and divided "Thou shalt not covet" into two commandments, one concerning people and the other concerning things.

Law and Gospel

Christians consider that Jesus Christ reinterpreted the law and in living, dying, and rising again fulfilled it. A great part of the Sermon on the Mount in Matthew, for example, refers to these Ten Words and warns believers to keep them and even to extend the meaning of them. Do not kill prohibits anger; do not commit adultery forbids lustful feelings. Christians should be more scrupulous than others in keeping the law.

The letters of Paul and other New Testament writings also had much to say about the law. Paul contrasted law and gospel in almost every letter. In the letter to the Galatians, for example, Paul said that "the law was our custodian until Christ came, that we might be justified by faith" (3:24). Paul urged the Christians in Galatia to love one another, "For the whole law is fulfilled in one word, 'you shall love your neighbor as yourself'" (5:14).

Protestant Christians have stressed these teachings, and we have emphasized that Christ alone fulfilled the law. Whether in the Old or New Testament, obedience to the law consisted of both individual and corporate actions and allegiances. Prohibitions of murder and theft, profanation and lying, adultery and coveting, were joined with requirements for honoring God alone, honoring parents, and keeping the Sabbath: restraints. Social structures were designed to reinforce personal habits in following the law.

Law, Grace, Duty, Love

Reformed Christianity has paid attention to all scripture, the Old as well as the New Testament. The effort to hear the whole Bible led John Calvin beyond what Martin Luther had considered the proper role of the law, to constrain the wicked and to bring sinners to repentance. Calvin said the moral law, centered in the Ten Words, kept serving as a guide for Christians. According to Calvin, no one has thus far "attained to such wisdom as to be unable, from the daily instruction of the law, to make fresh progress toward a purer knowledge of the divine will."

The law helped people see God's will and aided them in following it, even though only Jesus Christ could save them. "The saints must press on," Calvin declared, "for, however eagerly they may in accordance with the Spirit strive toward God's righteousness, the listless flesh always so burdens them that they do not proceed with due readiness" (Inst. 2.7.12).

The law did not contrast with the gospel for Reformed Christians so much as it did for other Protestant groups. Major statements of the faith, confessions still important for Presbyterians today, spelled out the Ten Commandments and their implications for living. In the Heidelberg Catechism, for example, questions 29–115 dealt with the Ten Commandments, under the section "Thankfulness."

Question 94 asked, "What does the Lord require in the first commandment?" The answer, couched in sixteenth-century jargon, began, "That I must avoid and flee all idolatry, sorcery, enchantments, invocation of saints or other creatures because of the risk of losing my salvation."

Both the Larger and the Shorter Westminster catechisms had similar sections, and both emphasized the relationship of law to God's grace.

In worship early Presbyterians read or the minister recited the Ten Commandments, and our practice of summarizing the law for guidance follows that habit.

Freedom and Slavery

Interesting, isn't it, that Exodus and the law go together? In our culture we usually contrast freedom and being bound to laws. We value free time, free relationships, and personal freedoms very much. We even admire some "outlaws"!

Down deep we see the relation between law and freedom as much more complex. Our freedoms are guaranteed in law, for example. Our freedom to speak, to assemble, even our freedom to worship all depend upon constitutional law. Scientists follow "laws of nature" in seeking to discover and invent. Writers, musicians, and painters follow conventions, schools, and other "laws" of sorts to create new works and imagine new horizons.

Who would you see as the "free" tennis player, the one who just begins, or the one who is well-disciplined and practiced? Surely the second, familiar with "laws" of tennis play in his or her very muscles and brain, has greater freedom to choose shots and plan strategy. The second player still has to play, think, and move well, in order to exercise the "freedom" gained. There lies the Presbyterian emphasis on the continuing guidance of the law—it aids, as Paul said, when the believer tries to live in response to the gospel.

The Sabbath, One Example

The fourth commandment, as we count them, told God's people to keep the Sabbath holy. Earlier Reformed Christians understood this to be a guide, and in several cultures they forbade all work except "works of necessity and mercy" on Sundays. They considered worship important and wanted everyone to join in. But they also believed the creation story revealed the way the whole universe had been made—with a resting Sabbath. Reformed Christians sought laws forbidding work and commerce, some of which still stand.

My mother can remember growing up in a Presbyterian family in which worship, family conversation, and reading the Bible and magazines such as the *Christian Observer* consumed the whole day on Sunday. I can remember my father refraining from work on Sundays, even though it could have been a good sales day. In many Presbyterian families in North America, the habits ran deep and some persist.

For Presbyterians those habits (or even laws) at their best served freedom to worship and learn. For many reasons such habits have diminished, and we may be the poorer for their demise. Of course, these Sabbath laws also became idols for many, who thought by making and keeping them they would be more acceptable to God. Friends have told me of deadly Sundays, in which boredom and resentment prevailed.

The Ten Words have much importance for Presbyterians. We can see the many ways we pay attention to these guides for living. And Presbyterian interpretation of the passage has been distinctive.

5

Shout to the Lord
Psalm 100

A church anniversary! It was the bicentennial at the Salem Presbyterian Church in rural Kentucky, to be specific, a celebration of their two hundred years as a congregation. Never a very large church, the Salem folk now number no more than 150, even with relatives and friends. But they sing with gusto. Full of joy and memories, the congregation joins in: "All people that on earth do dwell, sing to the Lord with cheerful voice. . . ."

Here in verse, as Presbyterians have done for the full two hundred years of life for Salem Presbyterian and years before that, we sing Psalm 100, the "Old Hundredth." It offers a wonderful treasure from our tradition. The hymn composed by William Kethe and the melody attributed to Louis Bourgeois became part of the worship of Reformed Christians as early as 1550. Kethe and Bourgeois were both refugees, living precariously in perilous times, but they rejoiced in song. We have sung the psalm ever since.

No wonder Presbyterians have sung the psalms! As Reformers tried to listen to scripture, they heard the whole range of praise and lament the psalms capture. John Calvin, who wrote careful commentaries on all 150 psalms, said that they offer "an anatomy of all the parts of the soul" (from John Calvin, *Commentary on the Book of Psalms*, vol.1, p. xxxvii; Wm. B. Eerdmans Publishing Co., 1949).

"There is not an emotion of which any one can be conscious that is not here represented as in a mirror," Calvin claimed. Then he corrected himself: "Or rather, the Holy Spirit has here drawn to the life all the griefs, sorrows, fears, doubts, hopes, cares, perplexities" of people. Mainly, though, the psalms present praise to God (ibid.).

For many decades of Reformed life, especially in Scotland but also in other lands, Presbyterians sang only the psalms translated into their own languages and sometimes rendered into meter. Isaac Watts and Charles Wesley introduced into English-speaking Protestantism a wider range of hymns and psalm paraphrases in the 1700s. These songs of praise made specific reference to Jesus Christ and the Holy Spirit.

Many Presbyterians fought the changes, as we are prone to debate and resist other changes. Gradually, Presbyterian psalmody became more inclusive of folk songs and the melodies of various nations. However, we should remember that the Bible formed the basis for Presbyterian singing, as it formed the basis of doctrine and ethics for the church. Psalm 100 gives a clear introduction to the scriptural songs, especially if we also look at those psalms around it.

A Love Song

I learned Psalm 100 in the King James Version, and most of that language stayed in the Revised Standard Version I use for other passages we study together. But my friend Johanna Bos showed me with her own translation that the words actually are quite simple and stark in praise:

A Psalm for Giving Thanks

Shout to the Lord all the earth,
Serve the Lord with gladness,
Come before God's face with jubilation.

Know that the Lord Himself is God
He made us, and we are God's;
God's people, the flock of his pasture.

Come into the gates of the Lord with thanks,
To his courts with praise.
Give thanks to God, bless his name.

For good is the Lord,
Forever God's devotion lasts,
and to all generations his faithfulness.

Give Thanks to God

What does Psalm 100 say? It calls on all people in all lands to praise God, to serve God, and to have faith in God. It recalls God's creation of the world, God's choosing of people, and God's providence—common themes throughout scripture.

Psalm 100 says that God is not only powerful, but that God is good, loving, and faithful. To say that God is both God and good can be sung better than it can be argued. In our minds questions arise about death in general and the deaths of innocent children in particular—how could God permit them? About "natural" disasters we ask similar questions. We even ask about God's power or God's goodness when we observe the seeming harshness of nature. But we do experience God as both powerful and loving. We can sing praises, even in the midst of our laments and doubts.

The context of Psalm 100 shows that the Hebrew people also agonized over matters of God's justice and care. Look at other psalms near Psalm 100. Psalm 102, for example, prays a lament, a cry to God out of human distress.

The psalm writer, in a prayer, says days pass like smoke,

bones hurt, and enemies taunt. Has God caused the humiliation and the injury? Even in doubt and cries of anguish, the psalmist summons praise and a word of confidence in God's final, good purpose for the creation. God will listen to the praise and overcome the hardships of the people. The psalm mixes praise with deep cries of anguish.

While it seems to us that Psalm 102 reflects the feelings of Israel after exile in Babylon, Psalm 100 no doubt formed part of temple worship at some point for Israel: "Come into the gates of the Lord with thanks, to his courts with praise." But both the worship and the work of the people could "serve the Lord with gladness." This mixing of worship and everyday life seems very important throughout the psalms.

Psalm 100 was used after the destruction of the Temple, the exile, and the rebuilding of the Temple, and it continues to be used by Jewish people today. The people of Israel did suffer enormously over the centuries, and their psalms came frequently from the periods of exile and isolation. We can assume that, as today, all the people sang the psalms—the women and children as well as the men, common people as well as priests.

Many of the psalms, as in Psalm 101 or 103, carry an attribution to David, and others bear the name of Solomon, Moses, Ethan the Ezrahite, or Asaph, a choirmaster. Many have no name attached. As with hymns of later vintage, some may have been sung first by believers with no special training in composition and then picked up and used in the worship of the people. Other psalms show careful grammar and even begin successive verses with each letter in the Hebrew alphabet.

Certain psalms, including 1, 8, 24, 103, and 150, offer especially succinct and beautiful words of praise, and many people have memorized these psalms. Although Psalm 119 is the longest, many Christians also commit it to memory. And of course Psalm 23 has the special words almost all know by heart.

Reformed Worship in Song

Reformed Christians took the psalms as their own. Could it have been they felt threatened as the people of Israel had been? They were a minority, and many of them were also refugees in exile, such as Kethe, Bourgeois, and Calvin. Remember, they took doctrines such as God's sovereignty and our sinfulness from scripture. Does it seem odd that they stuck to it for worship as well?

Psalm singing rose throughout Protestant Europe, as it also characterized religious singing among monks and nuns. But while Lutherans and Anglicans also included other hymns, Reformed Christians mainly sang the psalms. The simplest, prettiest of the psalms received immediate focus for voice and heart. "The Lord's My Shepherd," for example, was given several melodies during those first decades of Reformed worship.

One slogan of Presbyterians, *Ecclesia Reformata, Semper Reformanda*—"The Church Reformed, Always Being Reformed"—applies to our use of psalms. Colonial American Presbyterians fought over inclusion of such hymns as "Amazing Grace" by John Newton; they believed these hymns were "human" poetry.

The revivals in early America brought Presbyterians into contact with other hymns and songs of all kinds. Composers offered verses and tunes aimed at the "almost persuaded," whereas all the psalms had taken for granted that people knew God and arose in the faith.

During the nineteenth century, increasing numbers of Presbyterian women wrote lyrics and melodies for hymns, or at least they began to receive credit for those they had written. Elizabeth Payson Prentiss, in the middle of the century, still credited her husband with most of the work (as custom demanded at the time). Her "More Love to Thee, O Christ," however, gained recognition in her own name.

Through all history, Presbyterians have kept paying special attention to the scripture-based hymns, particularly those from the psalms.

At present, Presbyterians across the country sing in many different ways, with a wide variety of "favorites" and even a range of hymns they do not "care for." I am fascinated to worship with a congregation of Native Americans who use drums, with another singing in Korean accompanied by an organ, and with a black church using piano, organ, and hand-clapping. Churches in rural Kentucky, such as ones at Phelps or Gustin, can use shape-note melodies, and a Presbyterian church in a county-seat town in Georgia prefers its piano to any organ.

In all these congregations, different generations of Presbyterians will have grown up learning different "old favorites," encountering new hymns from other Christian traditions, and being influenced by popular songs, radio, television, and all else that shapes our culture.

Our Presbyterian Church (U.S.A.) has authorized a new hymnal, which tries to bridge both parts of our slogan about being Reformed, yet reforming.

Singing and Living the Psalms

Music in worship is extremely important, but the psalms have meant much more than that to Presbyterians through the centuries. Reformed Christianity has claimed that all of life should yield a song of praise. Psalms have served as touchstones for living, "serving the Lord with gladness." No wonder Presbyterians have involved ourselves so deeply in helping others, in finding out new things about the world, and in trying to live godly lives. Other passages become more specific in raising these issues, but notice that even this cultic Psalm 100, focused on regular worship, also views work as service of praise to God.

Psalms, through the work of God's Holy Spirit, make their way into our prayers. Hymns based on psalms become "songs in our hearts" for good and bad times. Honestly, the psalms do give sustenance as the Spirit enlivens those words for me.

The same story comes again and again from others. I remember a college chaplain who talked about his imprisonment during World War II. Isolated from others, he said he would have gone mad had not the psalms "been there" for him in his memory and his piety.

Committing psalms to memory is more than practical, however. As poetic praise, and with hymns based on them, the psalms function as a bridge to a spiritual reality prose seldom discloses. The love and power of God so frequently seem veiled, or even absent, for us. The psalms are gifts that invite us to live in that reality when we sing them.

The psalms also provoke deep questions for us, matters well worth considering. For example, Is the praise of God universal? Do all people praise God, whether they realize it or not? Reformed Christians have different responses to these questions, and the psalms assist us in grappling with them.

Again, consider the language of Psalm 100, and its use of words such as "shout" and "jubilation." Does our Presbyterian worship have the joy intended, or do we limit ourselves unnecessarily with our value on being respectable and orderly?

Finally, I guess we must wonder about the nature of God. Does God enjoy praise? How? What kinds of praise are most pleasing to God? How can we participate in those kinds of praise? We know the psalms form at least part of the best we can render back to God.

6

Whom Shall I Send?
Isaiah 6:1–13

"Down deep, I have this feeling." He spoke quietly and with real intensity. "I see the needs of people and I want to help. I've felt it before in vague ways, but now I think God is speaking to me. How do I know it's God?"

The young man's statement resembled those of lots of other people, but it remained distinctly his. We talked together about religious experience and about vocation. Mostly I listened, and he told me of talents and interests in teaching and helping others. Should he go to seminary? Should he embark on some other training?

He spoke of the influence of others. One member of the church he attended had taken a special interest and had challenged him to consider ministry. He also saw people he admired in teaching and in law.

It's a privilege we share, this heritage in Christian experience and a sense of vocation for all. We Presbyterians have focused heavily on both, and we interpret our own calls by comparing them with those described in the Bible and in the church.

"I Saw the Lord"

Isaiah the prophet recalled seeing God in a special way. He may well have been at the Temple at worship, though the words themselves only suggest it. The words do recall a point of reference, a time of crisis in the nation when a monarch died.

Isaiah's first impression, God's majesty, came with a sense of surrounding heavenly beings singing in adoration. The great hymn we sing, "Holy, Holy, Holy! Lord God Almighty!" doubtless was inspired when a Christian poet read of this song of the seraphim.

A second part of the experience was Isaiah's own woe. Unworthy, lost, unable to stand such a sight, the prophet confessed both for himself and for his nation. An experience of being purified followed, and a hearing of God's call. The message? A difficult one to deliver—a word of doom for unfaithful people and a sinful society.

The stark account of this experience remained in the mind of many who read it, even in the minds of all the Gospel writers who recalled Jesus having quoted from it (Matt. 13:14, 15; Mark 4:12; Luke 8:10; John 12:39–41). Isaiah's call bore an ironic twist, condemning people lest they repent "and be healed," the very process of healing in which Jesus engaged.

The call of Isaiah also finds echo in the religious experience of Saul of Tarsus. Acts 9 tells of the vision of blinding light Saul received on the road to Damascus. Saul repented, believed, received baptism, and became Paul the apostle. Note that in the Acts narrative, the words of Isaiah did not become those of Saul, but rather those of Ananias, a disciple in Damascus: "Here I am, Lord." To speak in human terms, Saul the persecutor of Christians became Paul the missionary through the work of Ananias. This courageous believer also received a religious experience and a special call.

The Bible is chock-full of accounts of religious experiences and of calls to the faithful. Other prophets received calls. Jeremiah heard God's word declaring "before you were born I consecrated you" (1:5). Ezekiel saw special visions from God for the people, and he heard religious messages to be shared with them. All interpreted their experiences as calls for special words and actions.

Isaiah, other prophets, and some New Testament figures experienced a word or vision directly from God. On the other hand, Andrew, James, and John simply received a call from the earthly Jesus to "follow me." Peter followed, for example, but he did not confess Jesus the Christ until later, according to the Gospels. Did these calls differ in substance from the others in scripture?

And what of the calls that seem to have come from other people? Timothy received an invitation from Paul to accompany him as a missionary (Acts 16:1–10). Lydia of Thyatira, according to Acts, became a Christian and sponsored a church when "the Lord opened her heart to give heed to what was said by Paul" (16:14).

Many more portions of scripture point in different ways to the calling of believers. Other passages tell of special experiences of God's presence or of their consequences. Among the favorites of Presbyterians have been Ephesians 4:1, in which Paul begs Christians to lead lives worthy of their "calling," and 1 Corinthians 7:20, in which Paul advised believers to remain in the states in which they had been called. Reformed emphases on "vocation" have depended on these admonitions.

Revelation and Religious Experience

Almost all religions affirm that God speaks and allows people to experience special times of knowing. Christianity has affirmed Jesus Christ as the special Word of God, God's Spirit, the special witness and comforter for believers. Reformed Christianity certainly shares more than it differs with beliefs of the rest of the church.

Presbyterians, for example, have considered the authority of the Bible paramount in evaluating religious experience.

Sometimes they have gone even further, saying God has ceased to speak in the very direct ways reported in the Bible. According to the Westminster Confession of Faith, for example, God's "former ways" of revealing the divine will are no longer necessary since the life of Jesus Christ and the writing of the Old and New Testaments (6.001). How does God speak to us? Through the Bible primarily, the confession says, and any other revelation should be examined in light of the Bible.

The Westminster Confession claims that Christians can possess an infallible assurance of saving faith, a gift of God's Spirit. Though it might be "shaken, diminished, and intermitted" (6.100), this sense of assurance amounts to revelation as well. The Confession of 1967 calls the life in Christ "the new life" (9.21) and says reconciliation marks God's revelation for us. So two themes come together in this sense of assurance—both extremely important for Presbyterians—vocation and conversion. Let us look at them in turn.

Vocation in Life

The Bible teaches God's care for every person, for everything in the world. God designed all for a purpose. This understanding of purpose and providence led the church over the centuries to develop monasticism, which was, according to its proponents, a "pure" way of being in the world, undefiled and free to praise God. Bible passages such as Matthew 19, the story of the rich young man, and 1 Corinthians 7, Pauline advice concerning marital status, deeply influenced development of orders of monks and nuns. The "higher way" of religious living was termed "vocation," and the word was extended in time to include also the priestly calling by some church leaders.

When Reformation men and women read the Bible, they saw everyone "called" to special Christian life rather than just a few called in behalf of all. Protestants spoke of the "priesthood of all believers." They also considered all callings that contributed to constructive human existence as callings from God. In other words, God first called people to become Christians and then also gave each special gifts for service that each person alone could give. In the words of our *Book of Order*, we believe in the "election of the people of God for service as well as for salvation" (G-2.0500).

"Vocation" in earlier centuries involved far less choice on the part of individuals than it has come to mean in recent decades. The vocational horizons of sons and daughters usually were limited by the work and social status of their parents. Though such constraints still exist, many of us in more open cultures have the opposite problem—we can become paralyzed by the array of choices set before us.

Indeed, a major problem for us Christians has arisen in the very success of our understanding of vocation in society. The word has become so popular, especially in referring to trades learned in vocational schools, that we seldom consider its Christian center in God's revelation. When we do think of Christian "vocations," we think primarily of the ministry and missionary work as full-time occupations. We revert to the ways people thought about callings before the Reformation.

If we pay close attention to the Bible, though, we see God working in all kinds of ways to enable people to determine appropriate work and witness. We see the call of one apostle through another, of one minister through a discerning of needs, as well as another through a dream interpreted. We also see the vocations of all believers as they function in some work that God plans for them.

How can we learn for our living from those examples? How can we honor the vocations of people and recognize God's call when it comes through others? These subjects need lots of attention from us, and we have God's promise of presence as we seek to respond faithfully.

Call of Ministers

A call to ministry does seem important indeed, and Isaiah certainly remembered a call as formative in giving him direction and energy for prophetic responsibility. I worry that anyone today would enter the ministry without a sense of God's intending her or him to be there.

Recently a retired minister told me of his career, serving small churches in the country almost exclusively. "I have had a wonderful time, and I see now so clearly God's preparation of me for that work: the farm family I grew up among, the model another minister provided, the first church where people gently taught me things a seminary could not." His eyes sparkled.

Ministry can be rewarding indeed, a chance to help others in all their living and dying, their growing in the faith and in their doubts. I worry that in today's culture we do not listen enough to the possibility that God calls some of us to ministry.

We may be like Ananias, hearing God's call to someone else for special service. Ananias hears God's call and then enables another to hear God's call. In a sense, Ananias is the evangelist for Paul.

We may need to challenge others in the church who seem to bear the gifts for ministry to consider full-time Christian service. We may need to support them, as early churches supported the first missionaries.

Conversion

Though Isaiah 6 and most of the other passages cited above portray revelation to those already seeking to be faithful, such passages also pertain to conversion of people. John 3, in which the conversation between Jesus and Nicodemus focused on being "born again," became another model for conversion.

Presbyterians have also sought the conversion of people to the Christian faith. In the words of a minister friend in Zaire, "We cannot have the presumption to refuse to others what has meant so much to us—a living faith in Jesus Christ and God's love for me in Christ."

Think for a minute about some of the great evangelists in American history—Jonathan Edwards, Charles G. Finney, Dwight L. Moody. All were Reformed ministers. In more recent years, perhaps scared by the shallow theology and scandalous lives of many so-called evangelists, we Presbyterians have frequently hesitated to tell others of our faith.

I joke with seminary students that we Presbyterians seem "saved by respectability," and we shy from asking others to join us in the Christian movement because we do not want to offend anybody. We should be true to our roots, however, which are evangelical. And the experience of Isaiah has served as one model for vibrant testimony to the power of the living God.

God in Control

Like other passages we have examined, this one centers on God's final control. Isaiah 6 speaks of God's special control over the life of the prophet. Some years ago, a Presbyterian minister named G. Campbell Morgan said the big question was this: "Can we see God on His throne?"

> That is the whole law of service. In order to do successful service I need first a vision of God enthroned. Have you this vision of God? . . . We can see the chaos. . . . National corruption, municipal rottenness, dilettante fooling with the problems of poverty that ought to be the problem of every statesman. But high over all earthly thrones is the Throne that never trembles. If you can see God on His throne, then that

Throne is commissioning you to take the evangel of the crucified Christ to cure all the ills of humanity. That is our message. . . . By the vision of Thine enthronement, by the matchless mercy of the altar and the fire, here am I; send me."

G. Campbell Morgan, *The Westminster Pulpit*, vol. 2, p. 306; Fleming H. Revell, 1954.

7

Pray Then Like This
Matthew 6:7–15

At a meeting in Stony Point, New York, with church officers, one elder told of her struggle with prayer. A pediatrician, Dr. Brundage worked in a clinic in East Orange, New Jersey. Her parents and friends advised her to work in a less risky neighborhood. She wanted to help the poor as well as middle-class children and their families, and so she stayed. Then one day as she left work, she was assaulted. The man not only took her money, but he also beat her severely. She awakened in a hospital, with a broken arm, a bad concussion, and some other internal injuries. "We were worried you might not make it," her friend and medical colleague told her.

Six months later in her usual place in the choir in the First Presbyterian Church of Caldwell, she bowed and struggled as others prayed. But as she listened and thought, she felt a burden lifted and a strange ability to forgive the man who had mugged her. Tears in her eyes, she whispered, "as we forgive our debtors."

Dr. Brundage told other members of the session about her experience. "Prayer came as a gift for me, and I have understood ever since just how real God's presence can be."

As we discussed in that retreat, very little about prayer can be termed "distinctive"among Presbyterians. But a Reformed emphasis on learning from scripture about worship and work extended naturally to prayer as well. From the Bible, Presbyterians came to depend on different kinds of prayer—free prayer, family prayers, private prayer, and corporate prayer. Though many passages helped in forming Presbyterian doctrine and practice, the prayer Jesus taught the disciples has remained the model.

Sermon on the Mount

Notice that the words of Jesus' prayer occur during the teachings gathered in what is called the Sermon on the Mount in the Gospel according to Matthew. The whole thrust of Matthew 5—7 is that Jesus Christ delivers a new, more comprehensive law than Moses had been given. The Beatitudes, an early part of the sermon, stressed the special responsibilities of disciples. They should be more righteous than the scribes and Pharisees, obedient not only in action but also in intentions.

The inner life of the follower and the outer life should be in harmony; the follower should not only refrain from murder and adultery but even from anger and lust. Followers should not divorce, marry those who are divorced, or resist those who are evil. They should love their enemies. Likewise they should not show off in piety or charity. Believers should avoid loving money and other things of this world. They should love God and have faith in God alone. Was all this instruction just language about life in heaven? It does not sound that way. Was Jesus anticipating a heavenly kingdom coming right away? Perhaps, but his teachings certainly used down-to-earth language and illustrations.

Could believers keep perfectly all the parts of the new law? Of course not. Faith in God, the intercession of Jesus Christ, God's grace—therein lies salvation. But as in the discussion of the Ten Words (ch. 4), so also in the Sermon on the Mount came guides for Christian living.

The Lord's Prayer

As a part of the Sermon on the Mount Matthew included some teachings about prayer, including the example we call the Lord's Prayer. Prayers should be simple and to the point, not for show. Interestingly, in the Gospel according to Luke the Lord's Prayer is in even simpler words, and briefer petitions are given (Luke 11:2-4).

The setting for the Lord's Prayer, Matthew 6:7, 8, repeats the themes common to every passage we study together—God's sovereignty and God's care. God already knows what you need. God cares for you already.

Then the prayer itself begins with praise to God. God the good and kind parent, not the distant ruler, may you be honored! How like Psalm 100, as well as most of the other psalms.

The believer's prayer moves to ask that God's will be done. This almost sounds like fluff, until we consider the implications. Jesus prayed exactly this way, according to Matthew (26:39), in the time of his own testing before the crucifixion. Followers who pray "Thy kingdom come, Thy will be done on earth as it is in heaven" sacrifice their own wills to God's will and ask that the kingdom come here and now.

To ask for daily bread seems a modest request indeed, when even other passages of scripture ask for long life and riches. But it goes right along with the rest of the Sermon on the Mount—especially with the warnings of Jesus against obsession with things and money (6:25-33).

I still have trouble with the assumption in the next petition—that I have already forgiven others when I ask God to forgive me. Is that a hitch in the prayer for you too? Different words in Luke lead to the same problem. And look at the things God needs to forgive, if we read the "new law" Jesus has been announcing.

Asking not to be tempted also seems easy on the surface. But do we want to live without sin; do we truly want deliverance from evil? All in all, the prayer is a demanding one for all who pray it.

We Protestants add the benediction because sixteenth-century Reformers thought it was part of scripture too. They discovered and read some manuscripts that said in Greek, in the margins, "For Thine is the kingdom, the power, and the glory forever. Amen." The Vulgate Bible, a Latin translation in use among Catholics, did not contain a benediction. More recently, Bible scholars have learned that the manuscripts followed by the Reformers were not as old as those from which the Vulgate came, and the earliest of manuscripts do not contain the words. But the benediction has become such a part of our prayer that we keep it in.

It seems ironic that Presbyterians trying to follow scripture got further from it in this case. However, the same may be true for all Christians who worship on Sunday. It may well be that most early Christians worshiped on Saturday, and that only with the acceptance of Christianity by Roman authorities did Sunday worship become the rule. Whatever the case, Reformers read of worship on the "first day of the week" in scripture and considered the practice biblical. Both illustrations remind us to be modest in our claims that we follow the Bible more closely than others.

What Goes On in Prayer?

A great Reformed Christian of the twentieth century, Karl Barth, began talking about prayer by saying it "is a grace, an offer of God." Barth found Reformed leaders consistently speaking of prayer in this way. In prayer, we "pray through the mouth of Jesus Christ," according to John Calvin.

In the Lord's Prayer, following the model given by Jesus, this intercession is obvious. But according to Reformed traditions, this same way of understanding extends to all prayers. "When we pray," said Barth, "we can only return to that prayer which was uttered in the person of Jesus Christ and which is constantly repeated because God is not without humankind."

If prayer is allowing Jesus Christ to pray in us and for us, it is also obeying the command of Jesus that we pray. Notice that the Lord's Prayer is just one example of Jesus' telling disciples to pray. Paul kept asking Christians to pray, also. We understand prayer as "doing our duty" as much as other parts of the Christian life are our duty.

Regular discipline in prayer, for Presbyterians, has been extremely important. George Buttrick, a Presbyterian minister, said that prayer has its own discipline (George A. Buttrick, *Prayer*; Abingdon-Cokesbury Press, 1942). He said the casual mind kills it. Buttrick also described much of the variety in prayer.

Kinds of Prayer

Confessions of Presbyterian and Reformed communions have usually paid careful attention to the Lord's Prayer. The Shorter Catechism asks:

> Q. 99. What rule hath God given for our direction in prayer?
>
> A. The whole Word of God is of use to direct us in prayer; but the special rule of direction is that form of prayer which Christ taught his disciples, commonly called "the Lord's Prayer."

According to that catechism, prayer consists in petitions, confession of our sins, and "thankful acknowledgment" of God's mercies. More recently, the Confession of 1967 has spoken of the praise and prayer of the church as adoration, thanksgiving, petitions, and intercessions.

While Presbyterians have put great importance on the confession of sin, we have also stressed the other kinds of prayer as well. We find all these kinds of prayer in scripture, and all form part of our communication with God. In addition, as we find in Psalms, prayer may question God and voice our struggle with seeing and doing God's will. These kinds of petitions we sometimes forget, but they also come from the Bible.

According to Buttrick, we need to find a quiet place for private prayer and a "faithful" place for corporate prayer. Only then can prayer grow into "friendship" with God, the goal of regular prayer.

Buttrick advises us to begin prayers with self-preparation in meditation and honor to God. Then we offer thanksgiving, confession, intercession, and petition generally in that order. He suggests we meditate quietly in between the sections in our prayer. Personally, I have found that sequence very helpful over the years, though sometimes I find myself in another pattern when in distress or just full of praise (ibid.).

Prayer and Life

Prayer for Presbyterians is also related to all of life. Historically, worship and devotion have brought leaders into the world for service rather than taking them out of the world. Prayer moves the Reformed Christian generally into activity as well as into conversation with God.

Perhaps that is why I find the prayers of others so helpful and instructive. I can see from reading the prayers of Suzanne de Dietrich, for example, something of her faith and learn from following her patterns in prayer. The same is true of prayers of John Calvin or John Baillie or other Christians through the ages.

Which is more Presbyterian—free prayers or those composed and read? Both. We have both traditions in our part of the Christian family. Remember that the Lord's Prayer lives for us as both—a memorized, set prayer, and a guide to the form of free prayer.

Some good friends, Herb and Mary Bell, come to mind when prayer for Presbyterians is the topic in class or in worship. They live joyful, committed lives and share in the congregation of which I am part. They are old enough that no one would blame them for slowing down, but both help others. They work for Meals on Wheels, for individual refugees, and for inmates at the women's prison. They also serve community agencies that help in peace and justice efforts.

But in the midst of turmoil and caring, both bear a kind of serenity that comes, I am sure, from a life of prayer. Life has not been especially charmed for either of them, but through their serenity they offer a kind of prayer to others in trouble. Over meals they "give away" something of their lives of prayer. They use simple, vivid, and intimate words of thanksgiving to God.

Now the Bells doubtless shudder at my using them as examples, just as Trudy Brundage hesitated to let me use her story as an example. We Presbyterians typically consider ourselves sorry examples in matters of devotion and prayer. Many of us really are sorry examples, but those who practice a vibrant life of prayer often are too modest to proclaim how deep and rich that portion of the Christian pilgrimage can be.

And the Lord's Prayer really does point to God's care for us and God's answering of prayers. It also points to God's provision for us beyond time and earthly life, which is the subject of another portion of the Gospel according to Matthew.

8

When Did We See You Hungry?

Matthew 25:31–46

"This area in Peru has little rain indeed." Bob Patterson was showing slides of his trip to South America. First, he put a shot of arid mountainous land on the screen. "But with simple tools and irrigation, here's what can happen." He displayed a slide full of green vegetation, where we could pick out fruit trees. "Presbyterian Hunger Program money helps some really energetic Peruvians turn the desert into a productive area."

Patterson, a professor of agriculture at a major university, seems uniquely equipped by knowledge and interest to help lead the Hunger Program. With a practiced eye, he helps decide how a portion of the money given in One Great Hour of Sharing and in other Hunger Program efforts will provide relief and resources for those in need. A Presbyterian elder, he took time to see some of the work the church supports and to judge the effectiveness of some efforts in Peru and in Brazil. Patterson's prayers, as well as his time and money, aim to feed the hungry.

Barbara Gilbert, another elder, serves on that committee with Bob Patterson. Owner of a farm in Wapato, Washington, she and her family live daily with questions of productivity, stewardship of land, and decisions about chemicals and seed. This experience helps her decide well about the use of Presbyterian resources for the hungry. Caroline Grady of

Orlando, Florida; Ofelia Martinez of Progresso, Texas; and other lay people, ministers, Native Americans, Hispanics, blacks, and white Presbyterians—all together they try to make the money stretch as far as possible for those in need.

What are they doing? They work as Presbyterian Christians in response to this passage of scripture and scores like it that explain our duty in the faith. Their work does not differ a lot from that of the millions of Presbyterians who join them in support of the Presbyterian Hunger Program, the most extensive such program in the United States for the size of the denomination. Staff at the Presbyterian Center, led by Colleen Shannon, help the Hunger Program alleviate suffering.

God's Kingdom Is Coming

Jesus, in the Gospel according to Matthew, speaks of harsh times coming. The arrival of God's kingdom, as we joke today, brings both "good news and bad news." The good news is that God's justice will exist on earth as in heaven (as the Lord's Prayer asks). The bad news is that those people who fail to orient their lives toward the kingdom's arrival will ultimately be miserable.

Matthew 24 offers a rather harsh view of the coming of the kingdom, a warning that things will not be "as usual." People are responsible as stewards of God's creation in the meantime.

Matthew 25 provides parables from Jesus concerning preparation for the coming kingdom and the wise use of gifts provided by God for work in the world. The parable of the wise and foolish maidens contains a surprise, for those who brought extra oil do not share it. The parable of the talents also contains an odd twist, for the one talent of the fearful sluggard goes to the person who had doubled the trust. Things simply will not be normal in the new era.

The Sheep and Goats

In that same chapter comes the promise from Jesus concerning "sheep" and "goats" at the final judgment. Both kinds of people will be surprised on that day—for the "sheep" cannot recognize that their ministry was to Jesus, the king. Nor can the "goats" tell that they denied the needs of God's anointed. The situation reminds me to ask, as one pastor shared the puzzle with me, "What will be the two first questions asked in heaven?" She laughed and said, "'Why are *you* here?' and 'Where's so-and-so?'"

I marvel at two things especially in this passage—that the judgment will be based on behavior rather than on doctrine, and that the actions called for seem too commonplace to take notice of. This sense in the early church of being obliged to act as Christians, and the sense that God cares especially for the poor, should strike us as obvious. Yet my penchant for focusing on belief and my natural blindness to those in need make the story startling. Evidently the same has been true for others for most commentaries remark on both.

This passage repeats the common theme—one more time. The judgment occurs under the control of a sovereign and caring God. This time Jesus Christ, the king placed by God on the "glorious throne," does the separating as a shepherd. The judge is the very one who laid down his life for the sheep.

It also helps to see that these teachings in Matthew 24 and 25 were given to the disciples, according to the text. Jesus did not offer this difficult instruction to the crowd that figures heavily in other teachings. Rather, Jesus spoke privately to those closest to him. It makes sense that Christians grow into ability to obey the law of Christ, rather than that we begin our Christian pilgrimage with all the ability to see the needs of the world and our meeting them. On the other hand, in the words of Paul, we may begin as babies with a milk diet; we do need to move eventually to a full menu, "solid food" (1 Cor. 3:2).

Again, this may be a good time to recall a portion of the Sermon on the Mount in Matthew. Remember that Jesus spoke to the disciples on that occasion as well. He had said, according to the Gospel, "You are the salt of the earth. . . . You are the light of the world." He told the disciples to let their light shine before others, "that they may see your good works and give glory to your Father who is in heaven" (5:13–16). The Christian becomes increasingly transparent, so others can look through the believer and give God glory.

Reformed Ethics

As the Presbyterian branch of the Christian church developed, leaders saw that life and worship form one fabric. Sound Christian ethics has never said anything else. The Christian trying to praise God seeks justice as well as love among people. And that goal extends to personal and social life together.

From this passage and the hundreds similar to it, Presbyterians came to value highly caring for the poor. In Geneva in those first decades, providing hospitals, nutritious food, and adequate places to live as well as education for the needy became priorities for the government and the church together.

In recent years, with an emphasis on individual choice, many have looked back with scorn on the Puritans (many of whom were Presbyterian). True to the present picture of them, Puritans did meddle in all the affairs of the community. Mostly they sought to bring justice to bear on everyday life, however, rather than to stifle pleasure. Poor people needed a rest, they argued, as well as Christians needing unimpeded worship. So they set Sunday Laws, which were sometimes severe. Public welfare of sorts began under Puritan direction because of Jesus' command. Most Presbyterian communions in all parts of the world have had similar goals.

In colonial America, Presbyterians lobbied for better schools, provision for orphanages, and places for widows to stay. In the new nation, Presbyterians sought those of like mind in other communions to begin voluntary societies to stop prostitution, house the urban poor, and help alleviate social problems.

Their greatest effort in the early nineteenth century was to free slaves. Different Presbyterians, white and black, tried in various ways to undercut and to eliminate the institution of slavery, and disagreements concerning slavery as an evil split the Presbyterian church in the 1830s.

The force of this passage and others like it influenced Presbyterians and other like-minded Christians to seek moderation in the use of alcohol in America, and then an amendment to forbid the making of liquor. Temperance and prohibition grew in part from real concern about the welfare of the hungry, naked, unsheltered, and vulnerable people in the community. Interestingly, even though many sense that the eighteenth amendment did not work to curb alcohol abuse, another neo-temperance movement is afoot today with slightly different emphases. One illustration of this movement is the founding of MADD (Mothers Against Drunk Driving) in 1980. Another is the adoption of recommendations concerning alcohol use by the General Assembly Council in 1986, the first such statement approved by the GAC since the mid-1950s (see *Minutes of the 198th General Assembly, Part I: Journal,* "Report and Recommendations on the Social and Health Effects of Alcohol Use and Abuse," 26.075-26.333).

Two marks of Reformed ethics bear discussion: the recognition of our complicity in the evils we seek to overcome, and the sense that each person and all of us together should improve in obedience to the law of Christ.

That we are all "part of the problem" by our sinful nature many Americans find hard to believe. We all tend to separate ourselves from the "sinner." Naturally, we find ways of feeling self-righteous. I remember hearing the testimony of a man in another part of the Christian family at a prayer meeting in Pasadena, California: "Lord, I thank you that I have been perfect for these past six and a half years. I haven't been in jail. I've been faithful to my wife. I haven't gambled. And I haven't drunk . . . much."

I enjoyed the testimony, for it shows a Reformed understanding of all of us. And our reading of scripture leads Presbyterians to consider that "none is righteous, save Jesus Christ." I sense the sin that grips me so fully, at least in my moments of honesty.

The sense is not just individual in nature, for I see my participation in human sin more widely. I resist higher taxes that might benefit schools, and I do not work enough to educate others to the need for better schools. I share in corporate greed and depend upon it, in the lower prices I pay for goods, in the property I own, in the pension plan I share. I help pollute the environment with the flying and driving necessary for work and enjoyable for recreation.

Such a perspective does not seem widely held in the United States, and it may even seem strange to some Presbyterians today. However, it does follow Reformed teachings.

Such a sense of our sinfulness I find comforting rather than depressing. It makes me try harder, rather than less hard, to overcome the sin. But it also releases me from thinking I can do it by myself, or that I will in this life be entirely pure. Rather, God's grace gives salvation, as well as gifts to help me improve in Christian obedience.

Third Use of the Law

In chapter 4, discussing the Ten Words, we saw how Presbyterians have made some positive use of the "law." In Galatians 3 Paul said the law had been our "custodian." Reformed leaders saw the law as working in three ways: first, convicting people of sin; second, keeping evildoers in check; and third, assisting Christians in their growth.

Guides do help us, they argued. And Jesus came to fulfill the law rather than dispel it. How do we grow in mature

Christian behavior? The guidance found in scripture such as Matthew 25 and the Sermon on the Mount (Matt. 5–7) helps.

If we remain sinful, we also can change and be transformed. A friend told me of his background. He came to church as a teenager because he liked a girl in the youth group. Her family moved away, but he stayed for the friendship of the advisers and others in the congregation. Gradually he came to pray and learn of Jesus Christ, he accepted personally God's love for him, and he tried to follow the Bible. He asked that I not use his name, but he now serves as a civic and political leader trying honestly to grow in the faith. That nurturing and guidance we see as the work of God, the love of Christ, the Spirit's presence, and also as this third use of the law. It does not compete with other sources of grace for Christian living. Instead it gives concrete guidance to us: care for the hungry, the thirsty, the stranger, the naked, the sick, the prisoner, the needy.

So I do not wonder that the Presbyterian Hunger Program receives serious attention from so many members, who gave more than $4 million, which went to relief and educational efforts in most of the fifty states and in more than fifty foreign countries (1988 figures). Nor does it seem so strange that thousands of congregations contribute to the needs of people around them. And the areas of involvement—seeking aid for refugees, prison rehabilitation programs, housing, aid for dependent children, hunger-related farm help—they echo the call of Jesus for us to be giving to others. Don't they?

We see Jesus Christ in the hungry, the refugees, the prisoners, the oppressed. But we also see Jesus Christ as the head of the one body, the church. That image calls for another Gospel passage—John 17.

9

God So Loved the World
John 3:1–30

Saturday morning, early, and the chores confront me—cut the grass, trim the bushes, clean the dog yard, stock the bird feeders, sweep the sidewalks, weed the garden.

On some days these are my enemies, but most of the time I find them friends, occasions for whistling a hymn, thinking, and sometimes praying. On this morning I bask in the memory of dinner with friends, Joe and Lynn Coalter, the night before. I remember the vitality of their children, Martha Claire and Siram, even more keenly than the good food and pleasant conversation.

I remember that I failed to visit Jean Combs, who recuperates in the hospital from pneumonia. And I completely forgot the Hiroshima memorial service last Sunday night! I had promised Arch Taylor I would go.

I remind myself that I need to write Nan, my grandmother, who must stay inside on hot days like this. We joke that she will outlive us all, but she talks of her death frequently and with some anticipation.

As I clean too many garbage cans, I confess more sins of excess than those of omission. A yard too big, cars too many, life too full of luxuries, amid the desperate needs of so many. The confession forms: "Forgive our offenses. . . . We have done those things we ought not to have done and have failed to do those things we ought to have done. . . . But Thou, O Lord . . ."

The prayer stays in the plural, and my thoughts turn to our culture—so consumption-oriented, so selfish and greedy in its values. The words of last Sunday's hymn play in my mind:

Hope of the world, who by Thy cross didst save us
From death and dark despair, from sin and guilt;
We render back the love Thy mercy gave us;
Take Thou our lives and use them as Thou wilt.

I wondered if Georgia Harkness, also a seminary professor, wrote the hymn as she did chores. No, she probably lived a simpler life, with no dog yard to clean.

The mix of enjoying myself and remembering others fondly, regretting opportunities missed and promises broken, admitting complicity in social sin, and thinking about things to do and Christian resources for the energy and discipline to do them—this mix characterizes my life. Does it also characterize your life? To this human routine as well as to times of crisis, the gospel of God's love in Christ speaks words of grace. Georgia Harkness doubtless put it better than I could, and her hymn of praise echoes John's account of the good news.

Gospel According to John

All four of the Gospels gained that name with good reason. They tell the "good news" of Jesus Christ. Reformers heard that gospel, as Christians had through the centuries. They stressed the total nature of God's gift in Jesus Christ, and they listened especially to John.

The Gospel according to John begins with an assertion—that the Word was, from the beginning, with God. Note that two other Gospels start with stories of the birth of Jesus, while Mark begins with Jesus' ministry. John describes the life, death, and resurrection in a more directly theological setting than the others.

Notice also a tension in the Gospel according to John between God's love for the whole world and Jesus' coming for those who believe in God through him. Jesus said, "I am the light of the world," and that people believing in him would have life (8:12). John keeps emphasizing both throughout the book.

John the Baptist plays an important part in the drama, by John's account. In chapter 1, John the Baptist introduces Jesus. In chapter 3, John tells his disciples that Jesus must increase, while John decreases, the model of discipleship.

Each section in the Gospel according to John tells something special about the nature of Jesus Christ. The wedding in Galilee, for example, showed Jesus' "glory" (2:11). The driving of money changers from the Temple, and Jesus' reference to destroying the Temple, foretold the crucifixion (2:13–22).

The material covered in chapter 3 appears early in the saga about Jesus the Christ to teach us more elementary lessons. It has two sections, by most accounts—a discussion with Nicodemus and the dialogue with John the Baptist.

Discussion with Nicodemus

A Jewish ruler came to Jesus by night. Why? To protect his reputation or for safety? Because he did not yet belong to the light?

Commentators call him "a representative figure" for Judaism, or for leaders in society. In Greek, the plural "you" is used in Jesus' responses after verse 10.

Nicodemus began by saying words of honor for Jesus. Jesus responded by telling a riddle: One has to be born again (or born from above) in order to see God's kingdom. Nicodemus puzzled over the expression, and Jesus explained the need for baptism and God's Spirit. Revelation would not fit into neat, philosophical logic. Jesus would be given for God's faithful people.

Footnotes in most Bibles confess the question of the translators: Does John 3:16–21 continue the speech by Jesus, or does it come as commentary by John on the nature of God's love through Jesus? The Greek manuscripts offer the words without marks to help. Some presumptuous translators use red letters there, pretending to know the words belonged to Jesus.

The force of the message is clear, whether the speech came from Jesus or the Gospel writer. God's ways differ from human ways, and we cannot understand everything, even if we are "rulers" of this world. John 3:11–15 surely refers to the coming crucifixion again, and to the resurrection and the ascension.

But Nicodemus had been brought to Jesus by the power of the "signs" and respected Jesus for his power. Jesus' response: You haven't seen anything yet! Think about the wind. Think about God's Spirit. (Spirit and wind are the same word in the Greek language in which the Gospel was written.)

Veiled phrases, words with double meaning, riddles. The work of God cannot be "explained" in the usual sense of that word. Like newly born infants, believers must trust in God and depend upon Jesus Christ as truly savior. Born anew. Born again. The power for such a miracle comes only from God's Spirit, not our logic.

John 3:16 makes the more straightforward statement of the Gospel. John 3:17, equally important for the Reformers, keeps that tension between individual salvation and redemption of the whole creation.

Jesus and John the Baptist

The whole work of John the Baptist prepared for the coming of Jesus the Christ. In fact, the whole life of Israel "looked forward" to the messiah, to whom God would give "all things." Here was the culmination of the covenant, now extended to all people who believed. This looking forward—to Jesus' death, but even more to the full revelation of God in the resurrected Christ—becomes a lesson in this section.

Gospel Joy

C. S. Lewis, English Christian essayist, spoke of being "surprized by joy." He played on the phrase, for he told of loving a woman named Joy as well as of his conversion into faith. Christians through the centuries have been surprised by joy, coming to see that God so loved them that Jesus came for them (us). Even the faith we must possess we see is God given, through the Spirit of God.

The alternatives—to think we can earn salvation, that there is no salvation, or that we do not need salvation—seem to be perennial. In the sixteenth century, religious people had slipped into trying to earn it, from all accounts. Reformers were surprised by joy—Luther especially—that God's grace alone saved. In John 3:17, the Gospel also speaks of saving "the world." Protestants, as all Christians, heard that and hear it.

Reformed Christianity grew from this same joy. No wonder John 3:16–17 has been so important for Presbyterians ever since. It is a gospel joy shared among all Christians, one we seldom fully enjoy because we are so frequently seduced by the alternatives. Nicodemus could not earn salvation, but God could provide joy for him and for all he represented, joy in the good news of Jesus Christ.

The word of God's saving work in Christ does not resolve the tension John's Gospel keeps—between God calling believers out of the world and God calling the whole world to redemption. But it ought suffice for us, in our partial knowledge and our condition as believing yet sinning Christians.

John Calvin said that God accommodates our situation

with knowledge sufficient for us. The Bible, in one way of speaking, is baby talk for us human beings who cannot yet understand all God's truth. But the truth of Christ is more than enough, and the Bible is plain enough in telling it.

Into the Light

Today we seem to have temptations other than thinking we can earn salvation. I suppose the most insidious temptation is to think we need no salvation. Even within the Christian church, I imagine lots of us think that way from time to time. I probably should not have been shocked when in an adult class in a nearby church, one man blurted, "Don't lay a guilt trip on me!" The class was simply discussing the responsibility of those with secure lives to help others.

Jesus invited Nicodemus into the light, into new existence. The person given new being in Christ does sense personal shortcomings and sin, but also God's redemptive power to heal and transform. In Christ, at special times, the world and people in it become transformed. We Christians can see sin and redemption where others might see only hopeless conditions.

That image of light helps, and Reformed Christianity has emphasized it. In Christ, life becomes luminous, full of a special light. I cannot talk easily of it, and my descriptions fall short of the reality, but conversations, reading assignments, worship times, and even doing the chores all bear special meaning and revelation from time to time. I assume that the process of seeing through the routine and the tragic to God's truth for eternity continues—maybe the Christian even grows more perceptive—as faith continues.

Presbyterians talk about the process as "sanctification." We grow into the light. And though I know we cannot judge others' progression in the Christian life, still I can see over decades real growth in Christian friends. An aunt and uncle, always good Christians in my book, seem in recent years to have more wisdom in the faith, more wonder at the beauty of the world, and even more compassion and listening power than they used to have.

Other friends where I grew up, Dr. and Mrs. Holmes, now live in a retirement home. I visited them recently, and I enjoyed seeing their interest in and care for everyone there. Dr. Holmes's prayer before the dinner we shared showed an intimacy with God's Spirit.

We Presbyterians back off from words about human perfection. We see ourselves embroiled in sin—even the best of us. Yet we believe "God so loved the world . . ."

10

Keep Them in Thy Name
John 17

Worship again, this time with the Edisto Presbyterian Church on one of the Sea Islands of South Carolina. Men and women, boys and girls gather—all ages. Announcements call attention to the special needs of members of the congregation, and the sermon, based on the Gospel according to John, asks everyone to consider the suffering love of Jesus Christ. Very special and yet quite routine.

I am drawn by the sense that we are one with people in general and with Christians in particular throughout the world. The prayer offered by an elder includes petitions for those in China seeking greater freedom, especially Christian leaders there. She also prays for people black and white and colored in South Africa—that they may learn to love one another and share in justice and peace. The preacher, in another prayer, mentions sisters and brothers in the cities and throughout the land who pay attention to the young and asks God's blessing on them. As they pray, I can even sense the presence of Jesus Christ in them.

An older woman sitting in front of me fiddles with an envelope, and I see it contains her food stamps. I look around and see others dressed adequately but inexpensively. Obviously this is a modest sanctuary, and I know that few black people in the Sea Islands of South Carolina have significant wealth.

Yet our first collection is taken for "the needy." I notice the woman in front of me contributes some money, having set aside her food stamps. The minister later explains that money from this collection goes to emergency services through the community center on the island.

Presbyterian? You bet! This is the way Presbyterians think of the church and the world—both in global and local terms. Edisto Presbyterian Church has contributed missionaries and volunteers from among its members, people who have served other portions of the church in other parts of the world as well as in the vicinity of the congregation. And the sense of oneness with all others in Jesus Christ comes originally from this chapter and its reflection of biblical themes concerning Christ and the church universal.

Jesus the Christ

The Gospel of John portrays Jesus as the Christ from the very beginning of creation. In John, Jesus accomplished miracles as "signs" of his divinity, gave teachings that are more theological than specifically ethical, and explained in some detail his relationship to God. In the middle portion of the Gospel Jesus prepared disciples for the crucifixion and resurrection he would undergo.

The Gospel according to John differs, though not a great deal, from the other three Gospels in telling about the passion. And the God portrayed is still the just, caring one of the rest of the Bible.

In the sections before the prayer of Jesus, John tells of the relationship of the disciples to the world—an ambiguous one. The Counselor (Paraclete, or Holy Spirit) would be with those who belong to Christ but would also judge those who belong to the world (16:8-11). The Spirit of truth would guide believers. Jesus the Christ would be present again fully to those who followed him, and they need have no fear.

Believers themselves would fall away and be fearful, however, according to Jesus in John's Gospel. Jesus would not be forsaken by God the Father. Rather, Jesus would triumph and in fact had "overcome the world."

The High Priestly Prayer

Commentators on John 17 point to three parts in the prayer of Jesus Christ: he spoke of accomplishments in the world and his relationship to God; he interceded for the disciples; and he asked God to care especially for those who would believe in times to come.

Note the importance of God's glory in the first part, and the way John portrays Jesus as having fulfilled responsibilities to glorify God. The purpose of God had been accomplished, and now Jesus would be received into the same "glory which I had with thee before the world was made" (17:5; see John 1).

The second and longest of the three sections is the prayer for believers. God had originally selected them, and Jesus had fulfilled the responsibility to teach them, to give them God's word, and to keep them in God's name. None had been lost except the one necessary according to God's plan. Now they should be one as God and Jesus Christ were one, but only God's care could effect that goal. Protected by God and enabled to be faithful, they could remain in the world and grow. They could be sanctified in God's truth.

The third section, a petition for those who would come to believe through the witness of the disciples, includes much the same language. God would need also to keep them faithful and to unite them, as God unified the disciples. "I in them and thou in me, that they may become perfectly one, so that the world may know that thou hast sent me and hast loved them even as thou hast loved me," Jesus prayed (John 17:23).

The Nature of Christ

From its very beginning, the Christian church had been struggling to explain the nature of Jesus Christ. The major ecumenical creeds, the Nicene and Apostles' creeds, are two of the most important documents forged in church controversy on this subject. Losers in church debates were some of the major heretics among Christians, as the leaders at various times sought to keep everyone united and also faithful.

In the Reformation, formers of Presbyterian patterns wanted to say they stood in Christian orthodoxy. They were not heretics, though they sometimes accused others of heretical teachings. They pointed to this passage and others like it to say that they believed what it said about Jesus the Christ.

Jesus Christ was one with God from the beginning, not just adopted as divine during his life. Jesus truly suffered and died, as John goes on to say, rather than just seeming to do so. To help in showing their orthodoxy, the early Presbyterians adopted as their standards for belief both the Apostles' Creed and the Nicene Creed. They also tried to outline in contemporary language what they believed the Bible said about the subject.

Presbyterian confessions have frequently called Jesus Christ "the Mediator" between God and humanity. As Word incarnate Jesus Christ remained fully God and fully human during his earthly life. This Christ, uniting divinity and humanity into one person, interceded in a way no one else could have done. Jesus Christ mediated love of God to human beings and mediated human response to God. In the words of the Westminster Confession of Faith (6.050):

> To all those for whom Christ hath purchased redemption, he doth certainly and effectually apply and communicate the same; making intercession for them, and revealing unto them, in and by the Word, the

mysteries of salvation; effectually persuading them by his Spirit to believe and obey; and governing their hearts by his Word and Spirit; overcoming all their enemies by his almighty power and wisdom, in such manner and ways as are most consonant to his wonderful and unsearchable dispensation.

The Work of Christ

In John 17, Jesus Christ obviously functioned as the "priest" for believers. Here he also serves as "prophet," bearing word of God's justice and God's care for the world. Here Jesus also shows himself "king," just as Matthew 25 says Jesus would be at the time of judgment. Those functions, John Calvin explained, tell us much about the ways Jesus Christ works for the church universal—as prophet, priest, and king. Reformed confessions and creeds have followed this tradition closely until the present day.

Thinking of Jesus Christ as prophet, priest, and king has proven one helpful contribution of Reformed theology. Another has been the focus on Jesus' work in reconciling human beings to God. Though other passages may have summoned the image more clearly (John 3:16, for example), this one certainly shows Jesus planning to offer himself as God willed for those who believed. Reformed Christians have drawn several images of the way this offering has taken place—images of a courtroom drama, of Jesus as influencing people by his example, of Jesus overcoming the power of evil in a cosmic battle, of Jesus becoming the ransom paid to free people from bondage to sin. These and some other images all come from scripture, and at various times Christians have focused on each of them. Frequently Reformed Christians have weighed the power of the various pictures of how Jesus accomplished the atonement and their work has helped people comprehend the care of God for them.

Whatever the image we carry of the way Jesus Christ worked, we hope that salvation applies to us. We have assurance that the Christ who asked God to save "those who believe in me through their [the apostles'] word" (John 17:20) will love us eternally.

Presbyterian Side Roads

If this passage and others like it have served as a kind of highway on which Christians have traveled and Presbyterians follow, it has also yielded some side roads attractive to some. It seems to me these side roads concerning the nature and work of Christ meander, and they lead folk astray. But it also seems worth mentioning at least two that still tempt us away from the main road—dispensationalism and fundamentalism.

Notice that the Westminster Confession used the word "dispensation" in speaking of Christ as mediator. In recent decades, some have believed that time is divided into three or more "eons," and they speak of the present time as that of the Spirit. Their idea, gathered from reading some parts of scripture and ignoring most of it, caused friction in the Presbyterian denominations during the first decades of the twentieth century. It still persists in some American denominations. But almost all Presbyterians affirm that all three persons of the Trinity work and worked throughout all time.

Fundamentalism arose as Presbyterians and others sought to identify simple beliefs as central for the faith. They opposed what they saw as a drift away from reliance on God, and they tried to set five things Christians had to believe. One major "fundamental," they said, was "the divinity of Jesus Christ."

Fundamentalists, perhaps with good intentions, missed the main road. Jesus Christ, according to the Bible, was fully God and fully human. The Nicene Creed uses the word "incarnate" to describe the nature of Jesus Christ. You can see the same "main road" in the use of the word "mediator."

Both of these side roads—and lots of others, too—miss the mystery and wonder of Christianity in trying to explain too much about Jesus and about God. Reformed Christianity at its best has not presumed upon our ability to know who Christ is and how God works through Christ and the Spirit.

By the same token, we Presbyterians seek to love God "with all our mind" as well as with all our heart. Historically, we have explored the ways the Bible talks about Jesus Christ and the ways we have experienced God's love through Christ. How can we balance our God-given curiosity and our well-deserved humility concerning human ability to plumb God's mysteries? That remains a challenge for all of us.

11

Apostles and Elders Were Gathered
Acts 15:1–29

"I went to General Assembly as a skeptic. To top it off, they put me on the committee for finance!" The man sat in the middle of the group, relating his experience of God's special presence. We had begun by discussing how the center of Presbyterian identity is in the Christian gospel, in our response to it.

"Let's talk about our own faith." I had invited the fifty or so to think about religious experience—how much of it might be called "distinctively Presbyterian"? One man spoke of a time he almost died. A woman told of a conference for young people she had attended some years before. Then, with a stammer, the older man in the middle told of being a commissioner.

"You know," he repeated, "a General Assembly might seem the last place on earth to sense God's presence in a special way, but that's exactly what happened to me. When we tried to form the budget for the coming year, I could just see Jesus there and all the millions of Presbyterians and others around. The vision kept me on my toes, I'll tell you that! I could see people depending on our decisions, and I could see our report on the floor of the assembly being taken seriously by everyone in behalf of Christ's body."

It should not seem strange to us that Presbyterians have

religious experiences at meetings of governing bodies, but somehow it still does. Have you been to a meeting of presbytery, synod, or to a General Assembly? With the local session, these bodies govern the Presbyterian Church. If you go, even when you have attended many such meetings, you will probably sense an excitement and anticipation unlike any other. Sometimes the meetings themselves become frustrating or even boring. More often they present opportunities to share in spiritually nourishing events. In a presbytery meeting, we hear the witness of a minister just joining the presbytery, the presentation of a committee on higher education or care for the poor, or the report given by a competent professional. But even then we seldom consider it a religious experience. Since the man's statement, though, I have found several occasions in which I sensed God's presence in full measure at such meetings.

We Presbyterians consider our ways of governing the church biblical. We look to all of scripture, but especially the Acts of the Apostles, as the authority for our structure. Acts 15:1–29 offers one particular case in which the early church "was gathered" to interpret the demands of the gospel for their time.

The Acts of the Apostles

Essentially a continuation of the story of Jesus begun in the Gospel according to Luke, the Acts of the Apostles follows the development of Christ's body, the church. As Acts 1:8 promises, the Spirit's presence led to witness in Jerusalem, Judea, Samaria, and to "the uttermost part of the earth" (KJV). It also includes an idyllic profile of the first church, describes how the church dealt with problems in the world, and tells how it made decisions concerning its work in the world.

Those trying to listen to scripture in the sixteenth and

seventeenth centuries considered that the organization of the church ought be a model of the true intention of God for its life. About 20 percent of the Acts consists of sermons, given by Peter, Stephen, Philip, James, and Paul. Those sermons also gave Reformed Christians patterns for emphasizing preaching and even showing how sermons should be given.

Though a portrait of an idyllic Christian community is given (Acts 2:43–47), much more space in the book has been devoted to less-than-ideal situations: followers lied when they told the apostles about their giving to the fellowship; a man tried to buy his way into church leadership; people wondered whether a convert was sincere; believers argued about how to designate "leaders" in the new congregations (note 14:23).

The main problem we all understand well. It is, to phrase it as a question, "What are the requirements for membership in the Christian church?" Since the great majority of early Christians had been Jews, and since Jesus had been a Jew, many followers naturally assumed certain membership requirements for becoming Christian would be the same—circumcision for men, for example, and promises to keep a Jewish diet.

On the other hand, missionaries such as Paul and Barnabas were already preaching "Christ crucified" at Perga, Iconium, and Lystra among Gentiles as well as among Jews. They baptized believers—had that not become the new circumcision? The way the leaders of the early church met this question is related in Acts 15.

The Council at Jerusalem

Notice that real difference of opinion resulted in heated debate and the call for a council. Important leaders from the whole church met in Jerusalem. James the brother of Jesus, Peter, Barsabbas, Silas, Paul, and Barnabas were there, and doubtless others of the apostles and also "elders." Peter gave the opening speech, in which he called attention to God's care and control (our theme again). God had called Gentiles and also given them the Holy Spirit. Besides, the law had been a burden none could bear. Finally, people came to salvation by grace alone (v. 11).

James waited until after Paul and Barnabas had described God's work in their mission efforts. Then he told the assembly that Gentiles need not undergo all the requirements of the law. They should, however, keep some of the dietary laws.

The book of Acts says, "it seemed good to the apostles and elders" to choose delegates and to send word of the decision. Notice that Gentiles at this point still are advised to keep some parts of the law—not taking meat previously given for worship of idols, not engaging in unchastity, and eating only animals ritually slaughtered. This truly was a compromise between the two "pure" positions—one holding that all provisions of the law held for new members and one holding that in Christ the law had been overcome and none of it applied.

From that point, the Christian church "took off." In fact, Acts 15 constitutes a watershed, according to commentators. Paul's missionary journeys, especially, signaled that this direction was the proper one for the time. (But notice that food given to idols and other matters of diet continued as issues for the early church, as 1 Corinthians, our next subject for study, indicates.)

Organizing the Church

Reformed Christians in general and Presbyterians in particular did not depend on just a few passages of scripture, but also on the overall sense of the Bible in forming governmental structures. Church structure should take into account human nature. For example, the Bible teaches that human beings are made in the image of God, "a little lower than angels," and full of faith at times. Jesus permitted human beings to become his "body" in forming the church, and the

Holy Spirit illumined the church. On the other hand, human nature is also sinful; no one is perfect except Jesus Christ. Even in Acts, the reader could see human foibles at work. The epistles in the New Testament showed lots more myopia and sin among the "saints." How could a church both honor the potential for faithful obedience to God and provide for human errors and sinfulness at the same time?

The Bible spoke of "councils," for one thing. The church held councils through the centuries. A council adopted the Nicene Creed, and other ecumenical councils had defined heresies nicely. At the same time, the Bible spoke of election of some representatives within the individual churches.

Reformed leaders interpreted the leadership by apostles and disciples at Jerusalem as similar to leadership by ministers of the Word and Sacrament in their own day. They considered that the power had to be shared equally, however, between such ministers and lay representatives in order to keep the church from becoming dominated by clergy.

Reformed Christians in most European settings thought the church ought be firmly tied to the state. In Swiss cities, in Holland and Scotland, and for a time in England they pressed to become the "state church," which was the pattern of Catholicism and the one that Lutherans adopted as well. Only some Anabaptist movements resisted close alliance with civil power.

Before the American Revolution, however, the Presbyterian side of Reformed Christianity was the established church in no colony. The church arose as a separate institution from colonial government. Presbyterians came to see advantages in having some distance from the state. So during and after the American Revolution most Presbyterians cooperated with others with different reasons for wanting church and state separate.

The result was that American Presbyterians formed one of the first "denominations," which was neither a state church nor a dissenting church. The Methodist Episcopal Church was also formed about the same time, and denominations have come to be the characteristic religious institutions of most newer nations ever since.

Moreover, Presbyterian willingness to share power between lay representatives and ministers influenced development of such practices among Methodists, Episcopalians, American Lutherans, and perhaps even among Catholics. Most newer denominations, such as the Disciples of Christ and the Assemblies of God, have also followed the idea of sharing power. Of course, those denominations have also tried to follow scripture in their organizations.

Governing Bodies

Presbyterians heard the Acts of the Apostles and other books of the Bible calling for dedicated, mature Christians to lead the body of Christ. On the one hand, each congregation should have the right to elect members to represent them. On the other hand, the whole church has the responsibility to exercise mutual discipline, making sure that faithful Christians led the rest.

Presbyterians recognized that "councils may err," and that groups of Christians can also sin, as individuals inevitably do. On the other hand, they had the audacity to say that a majority of duly elected, mature Christians speaking in an assembly spoke the will of God more surely than any individual. That mix of personal judgment and corporate trust has characterized Presbyterian government through the centuries.

The Presbyterian church's *Book of Order* looks to the Old Testament as well as to the New Testament in speaking of the work of the elders, deacons, and ministers. It also uses the words of scripture. "Elders should be persons of faith, dedication, and good judgment," says the *Book of Order* (G-6.0303). "Their manner of life should be a demonstration of the Christian gospel, both within the church and in the world." Deacons should be people of "sympathy, witness, and service after the example of Jesus Christ" (G-60401). Though all members of the church exercise ministry, ministers of the Word should be those "responsible for a quality of life and relationships that commend the gospel to all persons and that communicate its joy and its justice" (G-6.0202). Those are tough standards for leaders among Christians.

But the Bible sets those standards, and it spells out the nature of assemblies. Again, Old and New Testament provisions for leadership lead to responsibility and jurisdiction. Listen to the *Book of Order* on the subject (G-9.0102):

> Governing bodies of the church are distinct from the government of the state. . . . They may frame symbols of faith, bear testimony against error in doctrine and immorality in life, resolve questions of doctrine and of discipline, give counsel in matters of conscience. . . . They have responsibility for the leadership, guidance, and government of that portion of the church which is under their jurisdiction.

Sessions, presbyteries, synods, and the General Assembly may not be exactly like the council at Jerusalem, but they do offer shared power the way the Bible showed that council and other governing boards behaving. I enjoy watching good officers at work—caring for people and trying to listen for God's will in our lives. Governing bodies, as individual Christians, rest secure in God's grace and hope for redemption. The apostle Paul kept talking about that.

12

More Than Conquerors

Romans 8:18–39

They sat quietly drinking tea—the principal and the minister. An hour before, they had given rousing speeches to the seminary community, and now they both seemed a bit tired, surrounded by students, spouses, and faculty members in the cafeteria at school. They fairly radiated Christian faith, though, and their lyrical voices continued to instruct us.

"But don't the white South Africans also believe God is on their side?" one student asked.

"Certainly they do, most of them, at times," the minister replied. He served a congregation in Johannesburg. "And God is on their side—on every side—in one manner of speaking. I do not think all of them are damned for their ignorance and their selfishness. If that were the case, we would all be condemned. Rather I know God calls us blacks to freedom and full citizenship in the nation and the creation. If they stand against freedom for people, God will surely overcome them."

"Are you frightened in confronting the system?" another asked.

"I fear for my family," the principal offered. He served a high school in Soweto. "My wife and children are in danger, and I cannot but worry about them. In weak moments I am frightened, too. But I know surely God will care for me and my family, whatever comes of us."

These Presbyterians spoke to us, helped us learn not just about the apartheid system in the so-called Republic of South Africa but about Romans 8 and the rest of the Bible as well. They embodied the certainty Paul affirmed in the middle of his adversity—that nothing can separate us from God's love in Christ Jesus our Lord.

This was their first visit outside South Africa, and I imagined they would be afraid. God granted assurance to them even as they stumbled to phrase their perspectives. Eloquence came in their Christian piety, authority from the truth they spoke. In this conversation, they testified to God's power and love.

I have heard such eloquence and confidence from people in the hospital facing prolonged recuperation or imminent death. I have heard it from ministers struggling to serve God in the midst of the city. The certainty that God does provide for us is what Paul conveys in his letter to the Romans. I do not doubt that the Holy Spirit, at least in part, gives that assurance to people in need through a sealing of Romans 8:18–39 and other passages like it in our hearts.

Letter to Rome

The letter of Paul to the Romans probably comes first among the letters in the New Testament only because it is longer than the others Paul wrote. But it offers a kind of summary of the apostle's theology. Through the generations Christians have come again and again to see how important God's grace can be. Many leaders and ordinary Christians have found that message here in Romans.

Augustine, for example, read in Romans about God's grace and formed eloquent expressions of that grace, which Christians have found compelling ever since. Martin Luther, early in his ministry an Augustinian monk, read of justification by faith "alone" in Romans (1:16). Reformed leaders also depended heavily on Romans for understanding God's relationship to believers.

Paul wrote the letter to Christians, most of whom he did not yet know personally. He had determined he would start new churches, and therefore he did not want to compete with those preaching and teaching in Rome. But he did want to share in the worship and work of the Christians there (1:8–15).

Paul evidently wanted Roman Christians to help him get to the western parts of the Mediterranean world; for example, Spain. In anticipation of going to Rome to launch his efforts, Paul shared something of the core of what he taught (and would be teaching in their behalf if they supported him).

The letter can be divided into two parts—doctrine, in chapters 1–11, and ethics, in chapters 12–16. Of course, the two subjects overlap in the letter to the Romans as they overlap in all Christian thinking. Christian beliefs remain tied at all times to the actions Christians take. At any rate, the theological section of Romans centers on the difficult matter of understanding and accepting God's grace. People cannot follow easily the logic of God's demanding obedience to the law and then giving Jesus Christ as the fulfillment of that law.

The law finds both Jews and Gentiles "under sin," incapable of saving themselves. God's grace alone can impute justice, making it exist where it had not existed. All Christians can hear the biblical illustration from the life of Abraham. Paul cites Genesis 15:6 to prove his point: "Abraham believed God, and it was reckoned to him as righteousness." That occurred even before Abraham received circumcision. It depended upon God's gift of faith for Abraham and all Abraham and Sarah's descendants. The righteousness God gives to Christians does not entitle anyone to sin. Rather it calls from everyone the very best service we can provide for God. It's not that in this life we can ever be perfect! (7:21–24). Instead, God gives us life, eternal life, that we might walk in the Spirit.

If God Is for Us

Chapter 8 begins with a summary of the argument up to that point. Notice how personally Paul presents the theology—he describes his own struggles and joys in Christ. Christians have become alive through the Spirit. Such life opens a close, personal relationship to God, the loving parent. The whole creation will join in the new life offered through Jesus Christ. We look forward to this future in hope, and we believe it will come because God grants us that hope.

Even in struggle and suffering, we know God's control and God's care, that familiar theme. The Spirit helps in all ways. In our prayer, for example, the Spirit intercedes "with sighs too deep for words" (Rom. 8:26). God's providence shows to those with eyes to see and ears to hear another work of the Spirit.

Paul also declares that God's purpose has existed from the very beginning. God called those people who follow Christ before their lives began, and God will not forsake them. That word "predestination" occurs right in the middle of the argument. The believers chosen are finally glorified. Where is the evidence? In the life, death, and resurrection of Jesus Christ.

Does this mean life will be "charmed" for those who follow Christ? Absolutely not! Paul quotes from the lament of Psalm 44 to show that God knew Christian life would be tenuous. In trial, suffering, and even death, the love of God in Jesus Christ would more than suffice for Christians. Commentators say that the first list consisted of things Paul had already been through—tribulation, distress, persecution, and the others. The second list named "superpowers" that seemed to threaten the faithful. None could prevail over the love of God in Jesus Christ.

That epistle goes on to tell more of God's faithful and redeeming work in behalf of God's people through the centuries. Therefore Christians live in certain ways, anticipating God's kingdom that surely will come.

Predestination

Reformers did not want to talk much about predestination. Martin Luther usually managed to keep quiet about its implications, but he said it clearly formed part of the plan of God. John Calvin said it could be a "labyrinth," a maze that sucked people into a prison with no escape. Nevertheless, could a Christian ignore what the Bible affirmed?

Calvin treated predestination as one of the ways we know the benefits of Christ. It comes as assurance for us, like prayer and resurrection, especially when we are in need of assurance of God's love.

Reformed theologians could be tempted, though, to consider predestination a major avenue of understanding God's nature, not just understanding God's love for us. Moreover, they sometimes linked prosperity and predestination—those people whom God loved were those who thrived on earth. Sadly, such an "external" interpretation appealed to many, both Presbyterians and others. Finally, it became repulsive to most Christians. So we have a hard time understanding its original use in Reformed and other Christian doctrine.

We can read the Bible, however, and that helps a lot. That is the way "predestination" became a doctrine, because scripture said God cared for the people of God. In Romans, it is applied to those called by God, those to be glorified in eternal life—to the Romans and other Christians. It gives them comfort to know God will not forsake them, leave them to chance or to fate.

People in need, those struggling for equal opportunity in the world, hear the comfort and the assurance of predestination. It comes to Christians looking over their shoulders, seeing that the God who has cared for them throughout their lives will not desert them in pain or death.

To try to see from God's perspective truly captures us in the maze Calvin warned about. Here Paul says to look at Jesus Christ in order to see God's election of the church. Nothing in all creation will be able to separate us from the love of God in Christ Jesus. Is that not enough?

Mission and Hope

To the Romans, Paul offered a mission perspective. Presbyterians also took this perspective, from the life and writings of Paul as well as from the rest of scripture. Paul spoke of sufferings and assurances, grace and hope, that he and others in mission knew.

Again, as with predestination, the perspective can be misused and distorted. "We are more than conquerors" means one thing when Christians are persecuted and quite another when they (we) persecute. But the misuse of mission by some ought not to keep us from prayerful, hopeful, joyous mission.

Grayson Tucker, a colleague at the seminary and consultant for hundreds of Presbyterian congregations, has a questionnaire to help churches see themselves more clearly. "Find a congregation in mission, giving selflessly," Grayson says, "and you will find a healthy Christian community."

We Presbyterians have given enormous energy in mission, for those around us and for those throughout the world. We have offered people the gospel through establishing churches and schools, hospitals and model farms. We have worked cooperatively with other churches and sometimes with governments because we see mission in holistic terms.

We are tempted today to consider mission a thing of the past. Yet we have opportunities through our Global Mission Unit and lots of other avenues to share in mission. Our benevolence funds already support those efforts, and our prayers can help as well.

A few years ago, I was writing a book to introduce new members to the Presbyterian Church (U.S.A.). In that work, *To Be a Presbyterian*, I used examples of life from our own congregation—Anchorage Presbyterian Church in Louisville. At one point I began to catalog the efforts of members of the congregation to aid others informally, by volunteering and through serving on various boards of church and other non-profit service agencies. Just from my own knowledge I listed a couple of hundred ways in which Anchorage members served in various kinds of "mission" activities, and I could have multiplied that list had I begun to ask others of their work. Though I may serve only a few of these efforts personally, I really am linked in the work of others sharing in the body of Christ.

I should not wonder that Anchorage is a healthy church! Ah, but there are so many ways we could be helping, and we are not. . . . And Paul in Romans speaks not just of missions but also of eternal life. We will consider that subject in chapter 13.

13

This Is My Body
1 Corinthians 11:17–34

Communion Sunday in First Presbyterian, Franklin, Tennessee: We celebrate the Lord's Supper the way Presbyterians did a long time ago. During the previous week, the ministers and elders have examined all the members. "Have you committed any gross sins? Have you been studying to grow in the faith?"

Those who have passed exams hold communion tokens in their hands. Now we gather at tables for the Lord's Supper, depositing our communion tokens as we pass the offering plates. We hear the reading of scripture and the preaching of an "Action Sermon," telling us about the work of the Holy Spirit in consecrating the elements. "This is my body." The minister repeats the words of institution. "This cup is the new covenant in my blood." We eat the bread and drink the wine and pray together.

Sitting at table, with careful preparation, we become aware of this event as something holy—a sacrament. Truly, this is the body of Christ, the blood of the new covenant. I give thanks for those around me, for those who share the Christian life with us throughout the world. I imagine other times here in Franklin, when rural folk came to spend almost all day in a worship service like this.

My mind turns to the young people and children, of whom

there are many. I hope they will know the fullness of joy and peace in Christ. Christian communion—Presbyterian style.

As Reformers read the scripture in the sixteenth century, they also remembered and hoped about the Lord's Supper, and baptism too. They drew on the whole sense of covenant from the Old Testament, and they paid particular attention to the Gospels concerning the sacraments as well as to 1 Corinthians 11.

Christian Practice

First Corinthians is a letter at once very similar to Romans and quite different in nature. Many of the themes Paul includes in both letters—the love of God in Christ Jesus, for example, and the gift of faith in the midst of living. Both letters went to new churches in urban centers, where Christians tried to adapt the gospel in complex environments. Both letters undoubtedly came from the apostle Paul. And he expresses profound respect for the efforts of both communities of believers.

On the other hand, while Romans went to a church Paul had yet to visit, he addressed 1 Corinthians to people he had known well. Paul had helped start the church there, and he looked forward to going back to them. Moreover, "Chloe's people" had told Paul in detail about the everyday problems in this church. Paul's own authority had become one of the matters of contention, as had some earlier correspondence that Paul felt had been misinterpreted. So he wrote in response to specific problems, and he offered advice, for what it was worth.

Both personal and corporate problems confronted the Corinthian Christians, and Paul considered them partners in resolving those difficulties. The believers formed a "body," with Christ as their head, and Paul urged them to think of themselves in that way. They ought be "trustworthy," "moral," and "mature," caring for the faith of others as well as for themselves.

In this context, Paul criticized the Corinthian Christians for breaking into factions as they celebrated the Lord's Supper. Though that issue concerns us now, we should see that Paul treated it as just one particular matter among many in faith and ethics together.

The Lord's Supper

Richer Christians came to the special occasion of the Lord's Supper to eat and drink before the poorer members of the community could join them. Therefore some became sated and drunk while others remained hungry and thirsty.

To solve the problem, Paul recalled the message he had received and given among them—that Jesus Christ gave the bread and the wine anticipating death, resurrection, and the full dawning of the kingdom. If Christians abused it or fought over it, they did not truly celebrate the Lord's Supper.

Paul seems to have recited a set pattern for celebrating the Lord's Supper. Had these early communities already established liturgies and patterns for communion? Many scholars think Paul depended on such a memory when he wrote. Whatever the source, the passage became a standard for communion celebrations throughout the Christian church.

Questions for the Church

In response to this passage, and many others like it, a formal sacrament arose. Christians called it Eucharist, from the Greek word for "thank you," which people said upon receiving it. In addition, the "good favor" of God, another meaning of the word, called for human thankfulness. Gradually, to honor God and to respect the events of Eucharist, leaders observed more and more rules. By the time of the

Reformation, for example, only priests actually took the elements most of the time, and when the people received anything it was just the bread (body).

A "Mass" had developed, the name taken from the final declaration of dismissal in the service. It became one of the seven sacraments that existed as a system of worship in the Roman Catholic Church. So leaders and people questioned the habits of the church according to the Bible.

Why do we use words like "Mass" that are not biblical? Should we have sacraments at all, since the Bible does not use that word? If so, then how many sacraments should there be?

How about the Lord's Supper? Who should take it? How should it take place? Who should lead it?

Reformed Emphases

Reformers worried in the sixteenth century that people spent too much time depending on the sacraments for salvation and too little time trusting in God. They also disagreed violently on the nature of the Lord's Supper and the need for sacraments of any kind. Actually, more than anything else, different understandings of the Lord's Supper kept Protestants from uniting at the time.

Contrary to Lutherans, who still considered a "Mass" to be proper and the Lord's Supper in a way very similar to the doctrine of Rome, Reformed leaders said the celebration of Eucharist should be more open and involve the people more. It should not evoke images of a sacrifice by Christ, since that sacrifice had been given once for all at Calvary. Contrary to the Anabaptists and those seeking a radical reformation, Reformed leaders said it did remain a sacrament. Presbyterian understanding of the Lord's Supper has remained a "middle way" of thinking about it ever since.

The "spiritual presence of Christ" is with believers during

the Lord's Supper, according to Calvin. The Westminster Confession put it this way (6.167):

> Worthy receivers,outwardly partaking of the visible elements in this sacrament, do then also inwardly by faith, really and indeed, yet not carnally and corporally, but spiritually, receive and feed upon Christ crucified, and all benefits of his death.

Reformed people also worried about 1 Corinthians 11: 27–32, and they emphasized disciplined learning and ethical behavior as necessary parts of communion. That is why many churches in America and elsewhere used examinations and tokens to screen those who could "bring judgment on themselves."

In studying the Presbyterian churches in early America, I was fascinated to learn that "Sacramental Occasions," or extended communion services turned into the Great Revival, of the early 1800s. I should not have been surprised, for emotions would certainly run high. Gradually examinations ceased, communion services became briefer, and we came to current habits. We can see Reformed emphases still changing if we look around.

Communion for Children

Notice that 1 Corinthians 11 makes no special mention of children. Did they take communion there? We do not know. We do know that though many streams of the Christian church allowed children to take communion, some Reformers read Paul's warning (11:27–32) as forbidding children at the table. More important, as examinations and tokens disappeared, some Presbyterian leaders in the twentieth century considered that application of the warning.

In the 1960s and early 1970s Presbyterians moved to permit children at the Lord's Supper. I remember our own family playing a part in that change of thinking.

In 1970, we moved to Louisville, Kentucky, and began to visit churches. One morning we visited a downtown church for worship on a Sunday when they shared communion. Our two children, ages two and four, sat nearest the aisle on the pew. The elder distributing the communion elements naturally passed the plates over the heads of the little boys straight to my wife and me.

"I want some bread!" our four-year-old blurted in a stage whisper. "Yeah, me too," echoed the two-year-old.

"Shhh. Be quiet! We'll get you Cokes and crackers in a little," I responded.

"Why can't we have communion?" the four-year-old asked reasonably, in a louder voice.

"Shhh! Stop talking!"

To make a long story short, I began to ask the question for the frustrated children. Here I had a perfect opportunity to teach about the faith, and I had told them to "be quiet" instead. And did not Jesus fuss at disciples for doing just that? "Let the little children come to me..." had been the response of Jesus.

I asked my presbytery to overture the General Assembly: "Why can't children have communion?" After some struggles and some years, about the time our boys were confirmed and could take communion anyhow, baptized children were permitted to share in the Lord's Supper.

In the Directory for the Service of God (S-3.0500*d, Book of Order*), the invitation reads:

> The minister shall invite to partake of the Sacrament all those who are active church members or communicants in good standing in some Christian church, who trust in the Lord Jesus Christ and repent of their sins, and who covenant anew to live as followers of Christ. The invitation shall include baptized children who are being nurtured and instructed to participate with an understanding of the significance of the invitation to the Lord's Table and of their response in faith.

Baptism

Baptism is the other sacrament Lutherans and Reformed Christians retained, because scripture said it should be done. Both Protestant streams kept baptizing infants, as the Roman Catholic Church did also. Reformed Christians saw in baptism a meaning similar to the circumcision of infant boys in the Old Testament. They also believed the Bible, in speaking of the baptism of households in Acts, included children.

Later, a portion of the Reformed family became convinced that believer baptism was more biblical. Though Presbyterians generally baptized infants, most churches recognized the sincerity of those who resisted it on biblical grounds. Both ways of thinking persist for Presbyterians today. Notice the Directory for the Service of God provides for infant baptism and for believer baptism alike.

14

Behold, I Make All Things New
Revelation 21:1—22:5

"What should the new synod be about?" Leaders asked this question as presbyterians formed the Synod of Living Waters, comprising presbyteries in Mississippi, Alabama, Tennessee, and Kentucky. Responses came in from all over, and synod staff studied the results. The synod council appointed Jane Hines, a lay leader, and Wayne Todd, a minister, to draft a statement of purpose. Presbytery councils suggested changes. The writers edited their work.

In the fall of 1989, the synod adopted a statement of its "Visions."

We have a vision
of a world where our Lord's prayer:
"Thy Kingdom come
Thy will be done
On earth
As in heaven"
is experienced by all people.

We have a vision
of God's kingdom on earth where
God's name is sacred
and made manifest to all people in Jesus Christ;
God's power, wisdom, and presence are
acknowledged in all places by all people;

God's love, justice, and righteousness describe
the lifestyle of all people.

. . . .

And where we are led by the Holy Spirit into
The new Covenant
the new commandment to love and
A new vision.

The words of the "Visions" resound with images from Revelation and from other apocalyptic parts of the Bible. They mix naturally with those of the Lord's Prayer. Some people will doubtless think they sound "unrealistic." But leaders hope "Visions" will help in selection of such mundane things as educational programs and mission projects.

Every session, presbytery, and synod works in similar fashion—being granted visions of a kingdom dawning that enliven everyday life. The "visions" of Revelation have helped form Presbyterian visions through the centuries, though we may not have stated them in the language of the Revelation.

The Book of Revelation

The book of Revelation was written to remind Christians of God's care and final control over all things, which gives Christians courage in the face of persecution. A man named John is the writer, and traditionally scholars assumed him to be John the apostle. However, the writer John speaks of the twelve apostles as founders of the faith (21:14) and does not speak of his own apostolic authority. Moreover, scholars have estimated that the writing is from as early as A.D. 64 to as late as A.D. 125. Mysteries surrounding the "who" and "when" of the writing of Revelation go right along with other mysteries in the book.

Fierce and bizarre images fill most of the book. The use of such images was familiar to Jews and Christians alike from the book of Daniel, as well as from shorter passages elsewhere in what we now consider scripture. In addition, a whole library of apocalyptic writings had arisen from other times of persecution, and some still exist. The Greek word for apocalypse was taken into Latin and into English. Formed from *apo*, "reversal," + *kaluptein*, "cover," it bore a meaning all its own which remains today.

Revelation offers chiefly a vision concerning seven churches and their futures. The final vision of God's triumph in the creation, the reign of Christ, and the new creation give a kind of climax to the more particular visions.

Composed and read during Roman persecution of the early Christians, the book naturally treats Rome as the Antichrist or beast overcome. But no easy formulas or keys unlock the visions to give secret access to meaning. In the words of a colleague, Virgil Cruz, who studies and teaches about Revelation, "The author's purpose is not to present riddles which when successfully interpreted reveal dates of end-time events and the identity of end-time arch sinners. Rather, by means of a succession of often bewildering symbols, John speaks of the monstrous reality of evil, the certain victory of God in Christ, God's trustworthy promise to provide Christians with the strength to persevere, and God's call to be faithful in work and worship" (from an unpublished speech given before the 1988 Pre-General Assembly Planning Committee Conference of the Presbyterian Church [U.S.A.], St. Louis, June 6, 1988).

The visions concerning the seven churches—Ephesus, Smyrna, Pergamum, Thyatira, Sardis, Philadelphia, and Laodicea—told of their particular characteristics, but the visions also generalized on those distinctive things. Seals and trumpets, prophetic witnesses, and bowls all figure into the visions. How are they related? Certainly the number seven is important, as it is through the rest of the Bible. Maybe other correlations seemed important to the writer. But for us, it is enough that the tone of faith amid scary tensions and threats remains constant.

The New Creation

The vision of a new heaven and a new earth is a climax to the whole book. New Jerusalem, the holy city, is, of course, the church purified. The words of God, given in stately majesty, remind the reader of Isaiah's vision and call. But they now speak of an end time, in which people will be truly faithful, pain and death will exist no more, and God's presence in Christ will be full and fresh.

Again, as in Matthew 25, bad news accompanies good news. God's judgment will mean misery for those who were not true. Virgil Cruz points out that first on the list among those who "get it" at the end time, according to John, will be the cowardly—more culpable than the fornicators, sorcerers, the adulterous, or even the idolatrous.

For the faithful, however, a full experience of God's presence and power will be granted. Wonder of wonders! All the imagination can devise! Follow some of the images—God's radiance, like a rare jewel; the holy city of Jerusalem, with angels, apostles, and all the hosts of heaven; precious jewels and metals adorning the city, which has such true piety that the whole city is a temple with a light of its own, God's light. You could keep adding to the list.

Renewal will be part of the new creation, as will innate purity. And the reign will be eternal, so time will not corrupt things.

It remains a truly amazing vision, and it has inspired music and art, literature and religious experience through the ages for all Christians. The vision has also produced lots of nonsense. We can see how Reformed emphases help us in understanding Revelation, and we can see how important this passage and other apocalyptic parts of the Bible have been for Presbyterians.

Let Scripture Interpret Scripture

Although John Calvin wrote commentaries on almost all the books of the Bible, he never did one on the book of Revelation. I am convinced that he simply did not have time in his relatively short life to get everything accomplished. He used the book in his writings about theology, and certainly he was not afraid of it!

In fact, it has helped Reformed Christians in our visions ever since our branch of the Christian church began. We tend to seek God's will for governments and for nations. Here is a biblical vision that speaks of a "tree of life, with its twelve kinds of fruit . . . and the leaves of the tree were for the healing of the nations." The vision involves peoples and nations, not just individual souls. Presbyterians have sought purity in worship and work. Here is a vision that speaks of "the river of the water of life, bright as crystal" (Rev. 22:2), which flows from the throne of God and of the Lamb.

The power and pertinence of the vision have called us to think about the final goals and ends of Christian life together, as well as of our own personal lives and goals. How have Presbyterians interpreted Revelation? What has it meant? It has tested our use of all the Bible, and it has provided images of enduring value.

The most significant standard for following Revelation is the admonition of John Calvin—let scripture interpret scripture. God as revealed in Revelation does not differ from God in the rest of the Bible. Jesus Christ is the same, once for all, in the Gospels, in the Old Testament, in the letters, and in the Revelation to John. The same Holy Spirit that Jesus promises in the Gospel according to John and the Acts empowers us to hear Revelation and to hear "Come to me, all who labor and are heavy laden, and I will give you rest" (Matt. 11:28). In fact, many of the images make little sense without some knowledge of the rest of scripture—the tree of life, for example, and the throne of the Lamb.

Remember the second guide from Calvin—let the easy passages help with the hard ones. That is the general thrust of Presbyterian interpretation through the centuries. In that vein, the simple visions make the more complex ones comprehensible.

By way of example, look at question 107 in the Shorter Catechism: "What does the conclusion of the Lord's Prayer teach us?" See the answer? It "teacheth us to take our encouragement in prayer from God only." Notice that the authority for that answer came from Daniel, from Revelation 22, but also from 1 Chronicles and 1 Corinthians.

Christian Nonsense

Probably no other passages of scripture have been so misused by people of good will and by charlatans seeking to manipulate God than these from the book of Revelation. "I know the secret" is the game many Christians have played, including some Reformed Christians.

It is tempting to think we have secrets others do not possess, that we know secret knowledge. Moreover, the images of empires and nations among the beasts play on patriotic feelings. More Presbyterians have seen through these temptations, though, and recognized human limits in divine knowledge. Typically, Presbyterians have believed in eternal life but have devoted primary attention to the one we live on earth.

The nonsense of Hal Lindsey and his colleagues through recent decades, however, has tempted Presbyterians to shy away from Revelation and the other apocalyptic works as well. Sometimes we have used the passages only for funeral consolation. That, too, seems nonsensical. The power and love of God show through Revelation as surely as elsewhere in the Bible.

God's Care and Control

Recently a special committee appointed by the moderator of the Presbyterian Church (U.S.A.) has been working to draft a "Brief Statement of Faith" for our church. Notice how the conclusion has the same flavor of God's kingdom dawning as in Revelation:

72 In gratitude to God, empowered by the Spirit,
73 we strive to serve Christ in our daily tasks
74 and to live holy and joyful lives,
75 even as we watch for God's new heaven and new earth,
76 praying, "Come, Lord Jesus!"

77 With believers in every time and place,
78 we rejoice that nothing in life or in death
79 can separate us from the love of God in Christ Jesus our Lord.

80 Glory be to the Father, and to the Son, and to the Holy Spirit. Amen.

The statement from which the above was taken was unanimously adopted on January 12, 1990, by the Special Committee to Prepare a Brief Statement of the Reformed Faith (appointed 1984) and the Committee of 15 (appointed 1989) for submission to the 202nd General Assembly (1990).

15

The Beginning of Wisdom
Lots More Bible

Though we have studied twelve passages of scripture and something of their impact on Presbyterian identity, recognize how many more passages have affected our heritage. I asked some seminary colleagues and some serious seminary students each to list twenty portions of the Bible that affected our faith. Though most of the passages we have studied appeared on most of the lists, lots more came to their minds as contributing to our life together.

"The fear of the Lord is the beginning of knowledge: . . . fools despise wisdom and instruction" (Proverbs 1:7). That appeared on several lists, for it seemed to be one of John Calvin's favorite passages in all the Bible. Of course, Calvin understood "fear" as the respect of children for their loving, caring parent—not as cowering or paralysis in fright.

Many people picked Galatians 5:22–24 and other lists of virtues: "But the fruit of the Spirit is love, joy, peace, patience, kindness, goodness, faithfulness, gentleness, self-control." They argued that Presbyterians have concentrated on nurture, and these virtues have been guides in Christian growth.

Most named one or more of the miracles or signs that Jesus gave, according to the Gospels: Matthew 9 and the healing of the paralytic; Mark 6 and the feeding of the five thousand; John 4 and the woman of Samaria. The healing and the feeding by Jesus have had profound effects on our understanding of Christian ministry and of the special nature of Jesus, the Christ, as well.

They named other passages that have been important for forming our traditions, and here in the conclusion I use several more of their selections. But I also invite readers to make a list of special passages that have helped form your faith. After all, the influence of the Bible upon the church remains as important now as ever before. Here we are, claiming to change and reform as we have been reformed. God opens new horizons to us in the church and in this branch of the church we call Presbyterian. Surely the Holy Spirit unfolds new meaning for scripture and even new passages to influence us. What are some of those passages for you?

A Covenant People

Several faculty members and students chose Genesis 11, 15, or 17, or the whole account of Abraham and Sarah and Isaac. The sense of a covenant people began there in scripture, they said. Presbyterians have claimed that heritage in special ways.

Actually, God's covenant with people began even before that, with a promise to Noah in Genesis 9 that no flood such as the one from which Noah's family and the animals had been delivered would occur again. God also granted the rainbow as a sign of that covenant, requiring only modest dietary limits on the part of humanity.

The covenant for God's special people, however, contained more rigor and the expectation of obedience. Exodus 24—31 spoke of that, and Reformed Christians listened carefully. They separated moral law from ceremonial law, and they considered ceremonial law no longer appropriate.

Prophets called God's people to faithfulness in the law, and Reformed Christians have heard their cries. Several students named Micah 6:8 among formative passages. "What does the LORD require of you," the prophet asked, "but to do justice, and to love kindness, and to walk humbly with your God?"

Though we have focused on the call of Isaiah, several students and faculty paid more attention to the demands Isaiah conveyed from the word of God. For example, in chapter 5 Isaiah described a vineyard carefully cultivated but yielding wild, inedible grapes. The vineyard would be destroyed as a result. God said:

> Woe to those who rise early in the morning, that they may run after strong drink. . . . Woe to those who draw iniquity with cords of falsehood, who draw sin as with cart ropes. . . . Woe to those who call evil good and good evil. . . . Woe to those who are wise in their own eyes.
> Isaiah 5:11–30

Other prophets came to mind as well, especially Jeremiah. Reformed Christians were so influenced by Jeremiah that they even developed a special type of sermon called a "jeremiad," a condemnation of sins of the people in the name of God's righteousness. In the seventeenth and eighteenth centuries, when wars or plagues occurred, the people would declare days of special fasting and repentance, following the prophets' demands for obedience to God and promises of God's faithfulness to the people.

Presbyterians believed, and many of us still believe, that God chose us for special responsibility more than for special privilege. The *Book of Order* says, for example, that we believe ourselves chosen for service as well as for salvation. That comes from the prophets.

Biblical Wisdom

I already mentioned Proverbs 1:7, but the whole of the wisdom literature has had an effect upon us. The book of

Proverbs has made contributions to our everyday wisdom, and some of us still quote powerful admonitions from it: "Go to the ant, O sluggard; consider her ways, and be wise" (6:6); "A false balance is an abomination to the LORD, but a just weight is his delight" (11:1); "A soft answer turns away wrath, but a harsh word stirs up anger" (15:1). There are lots more! Industry, honesty, and tact have been characteristic traits of Reformed Christians, and an inclination to these traits was doubtless garnered here as well as from other portions of scripture.

Job, as wisdom literature, is especially valued by many. It may be short on explanations about suffering—in fact it critiques easy theology and cheap explanations of evil. But it has remained important for Presbyterians and other Christians because it tells forcefully of God's power and care. Ruth, the love story, is also important as a tale of faithfulness to God, whatever the results. Esther also has meant a lot to Reformed Christians for its testimony against idols, though it scarcely mentions God.

Gospel Teachings

According to the Gospel of Luke, Jesus sent out disciples and gave them instruction as missionaries. Luke 10 reports results, and Luke 24 follows with words of witness to the resurrected Christ. Reformed Christians, like others in the church, have found zeal for spreading the gospel in these commands from Jesus.

The evangelical core of traditional Presbyterianism surely comes from careful reading of John 3:16,17, but it also comes from Peter's confession, as in Mark 8:27–30. Several students mentioned that passage in particular. Mark offers the confession as a watershed for the ministry of Jesus, and others confessed as Peter had done first.

The passion narratives also have given existence and force to Presbyterian emphases on human sin as well as on the power of God to overcome death and sin. In this book, we have taken other passages for exploration not because they were more important than the accounts of Jesus' death and resurrection but because they teach more about Presbyterian distinctiveness. The passion passages feed all Christians together for the most part.

Pauline Theology

We have scarcely touched the power of Paul's letters for the Presbyterians. Reformed theologians erected a whole "economy of salvation" using the words and images from Galatians, Ephesians, Philippians, and the other writings by Paul, as well as those attributed to him, such as Hebrews and 1 and 2 Timothy.

They considered that Paul's theology "fit" with the rest of scripture, and that Luther's focus on justification came after repentance and mortification, before sanctification and life everlasting. The harshness of predestination, as well as its assurance, came from passages such as Romans 11:8–10; Ephesians 1:5; and 1 Corinthians 2:7: "We impart a secret and hidden wisdom of God, which God decreed before the ages for our glorification."

In addition, Paul's image of the church as the body of Christ (1 Corinthians 12:14–31) has undergirded the sense of oneness and unity Presbyterians have tried to embody. Paul's vision of righteous rulers and Christian duty has received a special hearing among Presbyterians, who read in Romans 13 and other such passages a "right to revolution" when tyrants tried to usurp the powers of God. The image of Jesus Christ as a priest in the order of Melchizedek (Hebrews 7) informed Presbyterian politics as well. On and on we could list passages influential in forming the distinctive as well as the shared portions of our faith.

Conclusions

We have examined several of the major passages that gave rise to a Presbyterian church. This church, or rather this part of the one church universal, grew from special emphases on the Bible and its place as a "guide" for our Christian living.

The Bible portrays God as caring for and finally controlling the whole creation. It tells of Jesus Christ, who, as the Word of God incarnate, lived and died showing God's love for the world. In the resurrection of Jesus Christ, God gave us a glimpse of the final overcoming of sin and death that will take place. We believe in God and in Jesus Christ because the Holy Spirit, promised by Christ, grants us that grace. That Spirit also bears us all the other gifts of faith, virtues for living, and hope for our salvation.

None of these major teachings from scripture can we Presbyterians call particularly Reformed, though the cluster of belief takes on a decidedly Reformed character when we emphasize God's godness; Christ's work as prophet, priest, and king; and the Spirit's accomplishing everything for us in Christ. This is also true as we emphasize the importance of the moral law as our continuing guide, the biblical psalms for our worship and prayers for our devotions, and the call of each of us to holiness and to vocations. Our Presbyterian heritage also shows in our learning from the Bible that God's ways are not our ways, that God's plan includes judgment as well as mercy, that the church finds faithfulness in representative government, that nothing can separate us from God's love, that Christ is spiritually present in the Lord's Supper, and that God's reign will finally come "on earth as in heaven."

John Calvin, when pressed to explain how scripture "works" for us, said it functions like eyeglasses. We can see plenty about God if we just look around at nature and study ourselves, he explained. But we are so nearsighted, we are like people whose vision is so poor they "can scarcely read two syllables" in a beautiful book. But if we have eyeglasses, we can "begin to read well." Scripture takes the blurry images and forms a true picture of God for us. We can learn from the Bible, because the Holy Spirit, the same Holy Spirit who led biblical writers to write it, helps us read it well.

We can also conclude from this study how important it is to keep reading and studying the Bible. That study needs to be taken seriously. We consider Christian life a matter of growing in Christ—"putting on Christ," in the words of Paul. The process of nurture begins with children, but it does not end when we become adults.

Benedictions

At the close of worship, a leader will provide a "benediction" for the congregation. Last but not least, most of these benedictions come from the Bible too. Some biblical benedictions are very simple: "Grace be with you" (1 Tim. 6:21b). Some we know very well: "The grace of the Lord Jesus Christ and the love of God and the fellowship of the Holy Spirit be with you all" (2 Cor. 13:14).

Let me close this book with my favorite, from the Letter to the Hebrews:

> Now may the God of peace who brought again from the dead our Lord Jesus, the great shepherd of the sheep, by the blood of the eternal covenant, equip you with everything good that you may do [God's] will, working in you that which is pleasing in [God's] sight, through Jesus Christ; to whom be glory for ever and ever. Amen.
>
> Heb. 13:20, 21, RSV alt.